Midwinter Light

Midwinter Light

MIDWINTER LIGHT

Meditations for the Long Season

MARILYN McENTYRE

BROADLEAF BOOKS
MINNEAPOLIS

MIDWINTER LIGHT
Meditations for the Long Season

For permissions information, please see the sources section.

Library of Congress Control Number: 2024932218 (print)

Cover design: 1517 Media
Cover image: © iStock / Getty Images Plus / Paper Art (Birch Trees) by Kheat

Print ISBN: 978-1-5064-8517-1
eBook ISBN: 978-1-5064-8518-8

Contents

2. The Wild in Winter

3. Soul Work in Winter

Introduction

Some of us loved Advent calendars when we were young. Some of us still do. My favorite form of this seasonal stash of surprises is a little cabinet with a space behind each small wooden door for a treat and (in our family) a little note—a quote, a love message, a poem. Giving a poem has taken hold among some of our family folk. On one recent birthday I gave an adult daughter a poem a day for each year she had lived. It was fun to find them and share them, and the poem that popped up in her email kept the birthday happening for quite some time.

My hope is that this little collection of reflections on winter poems, some of them specific to the Christian season of Advent, some simply a record of one poet's attentiveness to gifts that come in the "dark time of the year," will serve as an invitation to pause on each of these short days and let a poem open an avenue of reflection, as each of them has for me. Some may awaken memories worth revisiting. Some may inspire poems of your own. Some may lead you into prayer. May all of them enrich this season, this year, with words in which you discover glimmerings of midwinter light.

Marilyn McEntyre

1

RAINFALL, SNOWFALL, MORNING FOG

Invited Inward

> I would like to decorate this silence,
> but my house grows only cleaner
> and more plain. The glass chimes I hung
> over the register ring a little
> when the heat goes on.
> I waited too long to drink my tea.
> It was not hot. It was only warm.
>
> —Linda Gregg, "Winter Love"

When I first read this poem in the winter of the 2020 pandemic, it seemed to echo with striking precision two conversations I had had with friends who lived alone. Enforced isolation was a source of considerable suffering for each of them. It's hard to celebrate alone. Alone with our thoughts, we experience an unsettling nakedness and exposure of the self that remains hidden much of the time behind social and professional personae. Who we are with other people gives way to who we are, unadorned and unperforming, when no one is watching.

Isolated, with less banter, less back-and-forthing of opinion, no one to impress, no one to laugh with, we may at first feel the ache of diminishment as days grow more silent, "cleaner / and more plain." The tea may sit unsipped while the mind wanders and the eye scans familiar things we may not have paused to look at for some time: forgotten book titles that beckon from the shelves, the pleasing composition of shapes on the table where a small pottery collection has gathered a fine layer of dust, an artwork so long on the wall we have long since stopped seeing the layers of color and texture we once found stirring and surprising. Also, the empty chairs where visitors have sat, sated after a shared meal, and told stories. Threads of those stories dangle in the air like mobiles. Images from memory and dream collide and reconfigure themselves.

Winter at any time invites us inward. The liturgical seasons of Advent and Christmas lift up a story longer and larger than our own. Stars assume heightened significance and the ambient quiet of snowscapes, where we have them, stills us. Firelight holds our gaze long after we've let half-read books drop into our laps. Glass chimes that "ring a little when the heat goes on" offer their intimate consolation for loss of carolers and congregational singing.

It may be that melancholy befits winter and bears its own fruit. Like the wise man who came bearing myrrh, a funeral spice, the signifiers of death have a place among the festivities that come in the dark time of the year. Hibernation, cold, and dormancy have their dangers. Some will not survive. "I had seen birth and death," T. S. Eliot writes in "The Journey of the Magi," "but thought they were different." As, of course, they are, but more like one another than we generally acknowledge: a precarious waiting, unknowing; surrender to natural forces and rhythms; lives changed utterly.

At the end of Gregg's poem, the speaker realizes she has waited too long to drink her tea. Now it is "only warm," hardly offering the pleasures of anticipation and comfort that course through us with the first sip from a fresh pot. She will, we imagine, drink it, nevertheless. Warmth, this day, may need to be enough.

We live with less when the world grows cold and quiet, but less-ening is a lesson: we can live with less. We need the silences that allow us to hear small glass chimes. And simple warmth can offer an occasion to be grateful for small things. "All great spirituality teaches about letting go of what you don't need and who you are not," Richard Rohr writes. "Then, when you can get little enough and naked enough and poor enough, you'll find that the little place where you really are is ironically more than enough and is all that you need. In that place, you will have nothing to prove to anybody and nothing to protect. That place is called freedom." In that sense, "Winter Love" is a poem about freedom—about what comes after relinquishment and resides in simple contentment with a cup of warm tea.

Blue Christmas

Is it just winter
or is this worse.
Is this the year
when outer damp
obscures a deeper curse
that spring can't fix,
when gears that
turn the earth
won't shift the view,
when clouds won't lift
though all the skies
go blue.

—Kay Ryan, "Winter Fear"

Some churches, on the longest night of the year, hold a "Blue Christmas" service whose purpose is to recognize and offer consolation to those who have lost loved ones over the course of the year, and who are spending their first holiday season without them. Some, on those occasions, explicitly include those who suffer (as many do) from deepened depression, seasonal affective disorder, or simply the miscellaneous sorrows that come in seasons of festivity when life is hard and cold, and money is scarce, and the gap between prescribed celebration and strained circumstances grows wide.

Kay Ryan's poem testifies to the free-floating feeling of dread that often comes with sorrow, depression, or just the lingering melancholia that is a common feature of winter isolation and inactivity. That the inner world responds to and mirrors the outer world, the same forces moving through both, is a defining idea in romantic poetry but also, more recently, a documented fact in psychological literature that acknowledges how changing seasons affect our moods, emotional resilience, and the way we frame our inner narratives.

Winter dormancy looks like death. Bare branches and buried earth, passersby hooded and hurried on cold days, and recently, when the weather patterns are behaving oddly, the looming question of what climate change has wrought bring up for many of us questions that come from deep awareness of our own vulnerabilities: What if the things that have gone don't come back? What if this time, this year, is different? What if we're at the edge of apocalypse?

That last question gains currency among young people from time to time. My parents' generation raised it after Hiroshima. My generation reconsidered it after three assassinations, televised wars, and 9/11. One of the adolescents I love takes unnerving pleasure these days in dystopian novels. So do his friends. He's not a depressed kid, though he says many of his classmates are. His appetite for catastrophic, apocalyptic intergalactic warfare and mad scientists with nefarious purposes makes me wonder, sometimes, whether such story material is appealing now because young people are seeking ways to come to terms with the real threats they're inheriting. Before I dismiss such material for its bleak sensationalism, it may be that I need to consider its cathartic function, the paradoxical ways it offers hope, and certainly the needs it appears to meet.

We bring our sorrows into seasons of celebration hoping for healing, but sometimes find ourselves bruised by festivity that seems to deny the reality of personal or collective hardship. One challenge of the season is to find "midwinter light" during the very real darknesses people dwell in—the cold, the hunger, the danger, the fear. People of faith, people of good will, and people who can afford to be festive have no business being glib. I think often in this respect of Thomas Hardy's insistence that "if way to the Better there be, it exacts a full look at the Worst." We who believe in and have witnessed the work of grace can afford to take that full look. If we avert our gaze from the "clouds that won't lift," the bells we ring may sound a bit tinny.

At the Edge of Mystery

If you live deep enough within the heart
of woods, and wake just as the long night
begins loosening its grip on first light
and birdsong, you never know what might dart
across the fading screen of dreams.
This is the time when memory
is feral. Your eyes remain closed to see
your brother live again, then open to evergreen
shapes looming outside your window
that become your brother petrified
with terror at the moment death pried
him loose. You think you know
where you are, but are lost for good,
at home at last within the heart of woods.

                         —Floyd Skloot, "First Light, Late Winter"

Light comes late in winter. Even those who wake at a "reasonable"
hour find themselves rising in dwindling darkness. The temptation
to lie abed a little longer is stronger when mornings are cold, and

dreams fade more gradually before light comes to verify the solid facts of the waking world. Night holds us, this poem reminds us, in a "grip." Dreams hold us. Sleep holds us. Even birdsong seems circumscribed and contained in its chill bowl of stars. Waking, we break free—or leave behind the freedom—of "feral memory." A certain confusion is not uncommon in that waking moment, or perhaps just the paradox of our human condition: we are "lost for good, / at home . . .".

Inside that place, "at home . . . within the heart of woods," the mind receives a confluence of information from both worlds—conscious and unconscious—leaving us to sort it out and ponder it later and make of it what we will. As it was for the blind man in the Gospel whose miracle of sight returned only gradually, trees look like men, and appear charged with unsettling, evocative human presence.

Floyd Skloot's 2003 memoir, *In the Shadow of Memory*, tells of how his life unfolded after a virus left him with brain damage, including changes in cognitive and emotional functions as well as memory loss. The story focuses on his remarkable process of threading back together a sense of self, a picture of the past, and new strategies for living as a whole human being with cracks and fissures. This poem offers us a glimpse of the quality of awareness he has managed to turn to gift in his writing, riding on the crest of his own healing curiosity about the borderline experiences that all of us have at times, though he more than most. He is one of many who bear witness to the power and value of dreams. They remind us of mystery. They teach us that the conscious mind is only a part of what we live by, and perhaps not always the more important. They offer us information in images we couldn't have devised at will.

In this poem the dreamer's vision of a brother embodied in a tree, "petrified with terror at the moment death pried him loose," is haunting. Dream and death come together on this winter morning where the natural world lends itself to renewed awareness of human vulnerability, mortality, and loss. It is a time of day and year and a state of mind we may need to enter periodically to stay human—to stay humbly aware of how, in the finitude of this earthly journey, we walk at the edge of great mysteries, how there is always more to our stories than meets the casual eye, how information is available in strange and sometimes unsettling places if we don't look away, how love sustains us if we let it, and if we can accept that love sometimes looks very strange as we look "through a glass, darkly." Our love for those who are gone, for the creatures who sing in the heart of woods, for the body resurrected each day from the heart of dark sleep, for God—all those dimensions of love, and new hope with them, come together in hours and seasons of darkness and return us to daylight bemused, perhaps, but also amazed at how we are beholden and beheld.

Just Beyond Safe

The night is darkening round me,
The wild winds coldly blow;
But a tyrant spell has bound me
And I cannot, cannot go.

The giant trees are bending
Their bare boughs weighed with snow.
And the storm is fast descending
And yet I cannot go.

Clouds beyond clouds above me,
Wastes beyond wastes below;
But nothing drear can move me;
I will not, cannot go.

—Emily Brontë, "Spellbound"

Winter can be bitter cold in Yorkshire. And it can be hard for most of us who enjoy twenty-first-century household heating to imagine the combined effect of storm winds on moors, heavy rain turned to sleet, drafty fireplaces, and lack of insulation on even the relatively comfortable English middle classes. The Brontë sisters doubtless spent many winter days bundled up and shivering in their father's parsonage, tending whatever source of warmth they could keep stoked. They also wrote, as Emily does here, about wild, stormy hours on the moors—countryside that has become for many the very image of English romanticism—and a state of mind and heart defined in part by a fascination with what is wild in us and around us.

Storms are often metaphors for trouble: the rains came and the foolish man's house washed away; the storm at sea terrified the disciples. A dark and stormy night is a standard backdrop to many harrowing tales. "In the shadow of your wings I will take refuge, till the storms of destruction pass by," the Psalmist writes (Psalm 57:1). We need refuge. Little separates any of us from those we call refugees. Humans live in a limited comfort zone: too hot or too cold, we die. So a storm that bends giant trees, "their bare boughs weighed with snow," is a risky place for an unsheltered wanderer.

But the speaker in this poem is held "spellbound" out in the wild wind against all common sense. Something compels her that defies both convention and rational prudence. The notion of a "spell" suggests that what holds her is sinister or threatening—that she stays against her will. But in the final line her insistence that she "cannot" go changes to "will not go." She has chosen to stay out beneath the lowering clouds on the wastelands of winter fields. It may be that what binds her is not a demon's spell, but a fascination rooted in wonder—the kind of wonder that opens into awe.

We need that kind of wonder. We need, now and then, to stand in the presence of power the imagination can't fathom and mystery the mind can't penetrate. We need reminders that we are not in control, even of our deepest selves, each of us in our way fearful and wonderful and strange. Awe restores perspective and humility and gratitude.

The wonder of winter has been pretty thoroughly trivialized by incessant replays of "Winter Wonderland" in shopping malls at Christmastime. The cruise ship *Disney Wonder* where, according to the ad, "wonders never cease," is a place where "kids can immerse themselves in fantastical worlds only Disney could create." Real wonder, though, doesn't bedazzle; it holds us, expectant and vulnerable, in the presence of forces we live and die by—weather, earthquakes, waves, electricity, heavens that are, as the Gospel of Mark puts it, "ripped open." We are either terrified or exhilarated in the presence of those things—or both.

The speaker in Brontë's poem, whose words come forth in strong three-beat lines, interrupts her inventory of winter wonders with a refrain of resistance to the tug of prudence and the lure of safety. Desire drives her toward what she can't predict or contain, or maybe survive. Another English poet, W. H. Auden, honors this same desire in a poem that delivers a similar challenge to readers open to their own longing for connection to what is wild and infinite. The first stanza of "Leap Before You Look" begins with the startling line, "The sense of danger must not disappear," and ends with "Look if you like, but you will have to leap." The final line of the poem, after this prophetic word of warning to the timid, reminds us again, "Our dream of safety has to disappear." He speaks, of course, to those of us who take refuge in false comforts that numb and mollify.

Both poets lead us out to the edge of the comfort zone. Brontë offers us a glimpse of the infinite longing that leads us toward God. I know that longing. It's where real prayer begins. It opens a great space in the heart that nothing but divine Love can fill. Some of us, Brontë seems to suggest, need cold, windy, wild places to blow our small, domesticated hearts open to the "mighty wind" that cleanses our interior spaces and makes room for a Presence to enter who, like Aslan the lion, "is not safe, but good."

Local Truths

This is the snow belt.
This is the snow that falls
fretful as the flicker
of our eyes when we dream.
This is where people ache
along the road in their vehicles,
cursing each and every member
of the road crew
by name. This is the pin oak
in the front lawn shivering
all night, and sometimes
all day. This is the habit
of watching clouds
throughout the afternoon,
hoping it'll hold off
till we make it home.
This is the trickle of water
in the bathroom and kitchen
to keep the pipes from freezing.

This is the shucking sound
of neighbors out with their snow
shovels, people so thick
with clothing, and still
so cold. This is day after day
of school cancellations, and hoping
for once it would never end.
This is the old man
who sees angels dying
with the weather, and the old woman
who keeps putting him back to bed.
This is the joy of stillness
and the sadness of solitude.
This is the snow belt.
This is the belief
that everything has a reason,
even the tiny pain
that creeps through our shoes
and into our toes.

—David B. Prather, "Avalanche"

Growing up in Southern California, I knew snow only as a backdrop to stories by my favorite New England writers or as something you drove to and frolicked in for a weekend before putting your boots away and returning to school. We didn't have mudrooms. We rarely carried umbrellas. We have other periodic phenomena here: blistering summer heat, wildfires that are growing in magnitude, water shortages, occasional earthquakes.

Every climate system poses its own challenges and, I believe, offers its own spiritual lessons. We learn something about adaptation, endurance, resilience, prudence, protection, and compassion for the exposed and vulnerable from the earth itself, whichever part of it we inhabit. We are learning harsher lessons from it now as climate change accelerates.

"Avalanche" tells local truths. The most useful truths and teachings are local, rooted in the concrete particulars of daily experience. A theological term I've long appreciated is "the scandal of particularity." It refers to the incarnation of Jesus in a human body in a real and dusty place where divine revelation came to particular (and unlikely) people in peculiar and sometimes shocking ways. Those stories are scandalous only to those who want the divine to stay distant and incomprehensible and abstract. Poems, like sacred texts, deal in particulars. They point, for instance, to a man in his car cursing a road crew and the oak on the front lawn and water faucets and shovels. When they are named, those particulars both awaken memories and enlarge into metaphor.

Of course, the sharp cold that penetrates thick clothing isn't metaphor when it seeps into the body, leaving aches and tiny pains. Randall Jarrell taught me something about poetry when I read the final lines of his poem "90 North," and I thought of them when I came upon "Avalanche": "Pain comes from the darkness / And we call it wisdom. It is pain." Prather, too, insists that before it is an exquisite, glittering landscape, snow that comes relentlessly some winters is a weighty, obstructive, inconvenient, sometimes oppressive fact. It needs to be cleared off streets and shoveled off driveways and new boots need to be bought to keep toes safe from "tiny pain." When you begin with what the body knows, the truths you tell are less likely to evaporate into abstractions.

Another of Prather's poems, "Provenance," begins with these lines: "Everything begins here. And by here, / I mean this house, my house. / And to be precise, I mean the kitchen / where the morning sun rouses from the floor." Every action is the beginning of a story, every place a setting. Every noun and verb offer a place to begin—every spot where the morning sun rises from the floor. Stories and poems and epiphanies that begin in real places ripple outward into other places and sometimes widen into cosmic spaces. We inhabit eternity, but only because, as T. S. Eliot put it, we are "here, or there, or elsewhere." In winter, say. In the snow belt. A place where hope and faith assume shapes like snow angels.

Unwelcome Visitors

Hobo Autumn hoists his bindle,
hitchhikes out to another year, a warmer clime,
hoping to catch up with Spring—
then Winter arrives, demanding entrance,
banging at the door with cold fists as if he lives here,
doffing his hat to show where he keeps long nights—
when he opens his suitcase in the dank hallway,
darkness spills onto the floor,
a few icy stars roll across the rug—
he hands out freezing rain as if it were candy,
and from his frozen pockets he draws forth
a penny-whistle for the children,
upon which he blows a chill wind.
We give the old miser the extra room,
the one with the leaky window
where the draft comes in,
counting the days until he moves on.

—Jack Peachum, "Migrant"

Personification links us to the ancient world where every natural force was the purview of a god or goddess and nothing was entirely impersonal. It links us to the archetypes that give our psyches shape: the wise old man, the innocent young thing, the wounded child, the trickster. Personification is how we translate danger and deliverance for children. Wolves threaten and little pigs build houses and red hens grow frustrated. Personification reminds us to take things personally—nothing without intention, nothing outside the scope of love.

In this poem, winter is a migrant, a male visitor, not entirely welcome, invasive, intrusive, and inconsiderate. He brings penny-whistles for children but blows harshly through them, and hands out freezing rain like candy. He plays mean tricks. He follows his own purposes in his own time, and his story has its own pathos: He will never catch Spring, though he pursues her. He lacks the dignity of Boreas, the god of wind, or of Beira, Gaelic Queen of Winter. His power has dwindled, perhaps under the incursions of snow plows and expensive ski lodges and outdoor heaters and four-wheel drives.

But the speaker lets him in. His only choices, after all, are hospitality or pointless resistance. I think, as I read this poem, of people I know and love who live in places where winter is long, icy, sometimes threatening, and, slow to go, leaving a mess of mud behind.

I admit to romanticizing New England. I grew up, a bookish child, on Alcott and Thoreau and Hawthorne, imagining snow banks and dripping icicles as well as exquisite autumn woods and the breaking waves "dashing high" on the coast Longfellow immortalized. Later travel took me there, and to Minneapolis and Toronto and Boston in December, and I developed a new respect for those who weather the weather there. It is demanding. When we lived for a time in the Northeast the kids were delighted with "snow days," but more often were clearly not happy about rising at 7 a.m. to put on heavy jackets and boots and trudge off to the bus stop. I remember one of them saying as he ventured out into a particularly frigid morning, "This had better be building character."

I choose to believe it does. Character—compassion, kindness, patience, fortitude—is shaped and honed partly by what we put up with. We adapt. We reframe. We accommodate and adjust, and laugh when we can, over what we can't escape or control. Unwelcome visitors—even those with suitcases full of darkness—may be teachers. Receiving them we may, the writer of Hebrews reminds us, be "entertaining angels, unaware."

Letting In the Cold

The cold comes indoors with the newspaper,
an exact reading of the weather outside
folded into its pockets, cold, chilled
like a foundling too long on the doorstep,
blue after battering, like an argument
for original sin, no newspaper without
its built-in dread, and the one
exceptional heartwarming story.
Cold shakes out from the creases,
across the face, the knees, settling
at the body's mean temperature,
the smell of scorched food
pervading the whole house becomes
another odor domesticated, the smear
of fur & entrails on the highway is absorbed
by the wheels that keep passing over
and over it, and the newspaper turns
back into paper, our daily kindling.

—Kinereth Gensler, "December"

The news comes. We can read it or burn it or delete it. We can read it and then burn it or delete it. Or make memes for friends or write letters to the editor. Or glance at it, sigh, and decide to read it later. Morning coffee helps defray the cost of knowing what has broken loose out where fire and ice take turns teaching us our limits. After the reports from cities under siege and images of old women sitting in rubble, we look for the heartwarming story and huddle in it for a while.

Or we face columns of deepening darkness and enter the sorrows of the world. This is not necessarily morbid. Some are called to it, though there is no sin in healthy self-protection from what no one of us can fully grasp or solve.

News in winter comes with its own seasonal backstory. It's harder to be unhoused in winter. Heating costs are prohibitive for the poor. Tents in refugee camps barely keep the wind away from mothers whose breasts are freezing as they try to nurse. It's dark out there, and stark.

Even in a cozy home, comforts are more fragile. Who would we be if we did not feel a flicker of sorrow or shame or rage at the injustice that allows us so easily to nudge the thermostat higher and slide into soft slippers while not so far away someone on the street is feeling the cold seeping through rough layers of clothing, through skin and muscle and into the bone. The police will find her in the morning next to her shopping cart, lying on frozen cardboard.

Our prayers should be different in winter—harsher, perhaps, laced with outrage on others' behalf. Or watered with tears. We know we are small and easily exposed. Our protections are precarious. We live between 70 and 104 degrees Fahrenheit, some of us in food deserts. Shelters are full. Epidemics sweep through them, and common colds cause uncommon harm.

Despite the poem's unsettling images of winter's harshness—the foundling, "blue after battering," the "scorched food," the "fur and entrails" the highway absorbs, the most convicting, surprising words in it don't sound nearly so harsh: *domesticated, absorbed, daily.* The poet calls our attention to what we normalize, our thresholds of tolerance for injustice and inequity rising higher over time as we see them, sigh over them, perhaps send money or utter a prayer, and then turn the page, pick up the mug of coffee, and huddle back into our own protected spaces. It may be, he suggests, that the most vulnerable moment in an ordinary midwinter day might be when we let in the cold and the news for a half hour, perhaps, before we feed it to the fire that keeps us warm.

Water Is Life

Praise the rain; the seagull dive
The curl of plant, the raven talk—
Praise the hurt, the house slack
The stand of trees, the dignity—
Praise the dark, the moon cradle
The sky fall, the bear sleep—
Praise the mist, the warrior name
The earth eclipse, the fired leap—
Praise the backwards, upward sky
The baby cry, the spirit food—
Praise canoe, the fish rush
The hole for frog, the upside-down—
Praise the day, the cloud cup
The mind flat, forget it all—

Praise crazy. Praise sad.
Praise the path on which we're led.
Praise the roads on earth and water.

Praise the eater and the eaten.
Praise beginnings; praise the end.
Praise the song and praise the singer.

Praise the rain; it brings more rain.
Praise the rain; it brings more rain.

—Joy Harjo, "Praise the Rain"

For those of us who live in desert spaces, in lands of little snow,
rain is winter weather. After seasons of drought—for some of us
every long summer—rain is blessing. We share the dismay of those
who endure floods and hurricanes and sodden mud flats, but our
own sorrows have more to do with dust and desiccation. Rain is
restoration and promise. After a dry season it can seem almost
miraculous. The gray of midwinter is fully as beautiful as sky-blue
spring, and as full of life. Tribal peoples protesting pipelines that
threaten local rivers hold up signs bearing the stark prophetic
truth, "Water is life." It's not a metaphor.

A poet of the Muskogee Nation and US poet laureate, Joy Harjo,
deeply familiar with the wide dry skies of the Southwest, opens
windows for her readers into a way of life and a quality of aware-
ness urbanites may have consigned to a mythic past, but which
is very present and urgent, alive and available, if we are willing
to listen to those who preserve it. "Praise the Rain" invites and
enacts that way: line by line our attention is called to elements
of the natural world juxtaposed not by the rational categories we

learn in school—animal, vegetable, mineral—but by the ways they cross paths in the flow of life they—and we—share. All are worthy of praise. All are to be celebrated. The eye moves from the distant view of the seagull dive to the curl of a plant at close range and from the "backwards, upward sky" to the baby cry, uniting in a single breath what holds us and what we hold. Sharing a line "the stand of trees" and "the dignity" bring concrete and abstract, visible and invisible, together in generous equivalency: what we see, what we think, what we speak—object, idea, and word—are all real and present and part of the Spirit life that flits and flows within and among us.

The second stanza opens with adjectives—descriptors that become nouns when they stand alone: "crazy" and "sad" are also part of what is—states of being that deserve acceptance rather than judgment: each of them, perhaps, a stretch of the "path on which we're led." Some paths lead us through dark places; there, too, we're led. Harsh realities are enfolded in the repeated, insistent imperative that invites us into a kind of liturgical call-and-response: praise, praise, praise eater and eaten, predators and prey, beginning and end, birth and death, singer and song, the body and what passes through the body and dissipates again into the canopy of space.

All this praise, it seems, is brought forth by the rain. The rain that reawakens and renews, rain that Shakespeare made a sign of mercy, gently dropping from heaven, blessing the place beneath. Rain, when it comes, comes in sheets or fine mists; it pelts or simply passes by, dampening as gently as dew. It comes as it will, like the Spirit that "bloweth where it listeth." In these days of climate disruption, it may come in unsettling ways. But it comes unbidden, life-giving, life-threatening, longed-for by some, dreaded by others, signifying, always, that we live during givenness, drenched in grace by a Creator and created order that summon us in every ordinary thing to the threshold of mystery where praise is fitting.

Where Spaces Thin

Only what insists, sprouts, quirks
and angles escapes burial. Sticks
of blue and yellow peer and poke
from beneath encroaching white.
What has not given way—an old man,
a dog, a slanted roof that sheds the snow—
become the very things the hungry eye wanted.
They last, at least, are upright, and move
across the flat fields undisturbed by
all that has died, for a time.
—Marilyn McEntyre, "Van Gogh's *Landscape with Snow*"

Despite the curious term art historians have given them, ekphrastic poems have a long history. They are poems written in response to visual art works. Bringing words to images is the work of art and film critics and historians, museum docents, parents and teachers who offer small children words for what they see. Poets take up that task when an image awakens—as images are meant to—a feeling or memory or sudden insight. Over a period of several years, I made a practice of sitting with works by some of my favorite artists, Van Gogh high on that list, and letting words come. I was often taken by surprise; a half hour with a painting might lead me into prayer or into deeper appreciation of form and color for their own sake, or into new curiosities about the lives and sensibilities of the painters. It was especially gratifying to sit with a lesser-known painting like Van Gogh's *Landscape with Snow*—one that had not been endlessly reproduced on posters and mugs and tote bags—to see what might be made of its more modest claims on the eye.

On a frozen field one might casually describe as bleak, a man and dog make their way toward a stand of half-bare trees and a village in the distance. They are not lost in a dark wood; they are close, in fact, to company and domestic comfort. But in this moment, on a morning walk, they are surrounded by chill winter light and solitude and a thin layer of snow. Here and there the bare soil is exposed and thick stems of dormant vegetation line their path. The phrase that came to me as I gazed at it was "what survives." The second was "the vibrancy of blue." Neither of those phrases made it into the poem, but I was struck repeatedly by the vitality of the limited palette—browns, blues, and yellows gathering here and there into orange—and of how accurately the painter seemed to have depicted the unique quality of light where fallen snow reflects the sun.

Winter makes us see differently. Noticing is rooted in desires so easily satisfied in spring we barely feel them—for color, for movement, for the sound of birds, and things that bloom. On a walk in midwinter, we experience solitude in a different key. We are surrounded by reminders of mortality and loss, by the absence of what is lush and vivid. We are clothed in layers and aware of our bodily needs in new ways. And the quiet, sometimes, is palpable. It is a good time for prayer: the veil between this dimension and the next seems to have thinned.

The ancient Celtic idea of "thin spaces" has been revived in recent years by people who find in Celtic spirituality a way to hold in rich simultaneity all that makes us both earthbound and heaven bound. Some thin places are pilgrimage spots where mystical moments come more frequently, distractions fall away, and one finds oneself in contemplation, almost effortlessly. Sometimes a moment on an ordinary day becomes a "thin place" when suddenly background moves into foreground and heaven is noticeably present, in this moment, in this place. The Celts, we know from their legacy of poetry, prayer, and song, lived with a constant awareness of how close we all are to the communion of saints, angels, and spirits we cannot see. Many of us post-industrial folk need a little more reminding.

Walking in the natural world—listening to breeze in summer branches or to winter silences—can take us there. So can artists. Judeo-Christian tradition, among others, gives warnings about the making of images precisely because they are powerful enough to lead us into idolatry. They are also powerful enough to lead us into prayer, a fact that surely accounts for so many centuries of Christian art. Van Gogh's piety shifted during his well-documented sufferings—poverty, bouts of depression, isolation. But there remains in almost all his paintings a mute testimony to the way spaces thin when you fully inhabit them. The atmosphere itself becomes dense with energy, and distinctions among solid, liquid, and air seem less clear. Sunflowers can almost speak. The night sky is raucous with wild dancing, and even a landscape with snow appears to be a place where divine encounter could happen at any moment to a man and a dog in a field.

Singing in the Cold

The days are short
The sun a spark
Hung thin between
The dark and dark.
Fat snowy footsteps
Track the floor
And parkas pile up
Near the door.
The river is
A frozen place
Held still beneath
The trees' black lace
The sky is low.
The wind is gray.
The radiator
Purrs all day.

—John Updike, "January"

At first glance this brief, playful poem offers little more than a description of winter, seen and felt from the point of view of a person inside, where the radiator "purrs." The geographic range of observation is striking, both in its scope—going from the sun to the mudroom where a family's coats and boots are shed, then back out to the river and trees, up to the sky and wind, and back inside. The repeated contrast between dramatic features of land and sky and homely details of domestic life makes for a slightly comic effect: what we bring inside from the wild, harsh beauties of a winter day are "fat, snowy footsteps" and damp parkas. We retreat to the comfort of climate-control and the role of spectators at the drama taking place outside the window.

The rhythmic lines lend themselves to song. Reading them, I think of the widely quoted lines by the prescient German playwright Bertolt Brecht, writing about the task of making art in the face of what is foreboding: "In the dark times, will there also be singing? Yes, there will also be singing, about the dark times." The lines are from his "Svenborg Poems," written at the beginning of World War II about what was happening in Europe, seen from the point of view of a political refugee. Whether "dark times" is a metaphor for cosmic or global disaster or a way of describing personal depression or crisis or a more literal reference to the short days of winter, the poem invites us to sing in the dark times about the dark times. Rhythm moves us through things: marchers' stamina, and dancers', is enhanced by drumming. Laborers and enslaved people have sung to establish solidarity. Aboriginal people have "song lines" that take them from one place to another.

Songs of lament and hope provide the energy we need to "get us through."

As a song for winter, Updike's poem is neither lament nor celebration, but rather quiet observation from a warm and safe place of the muted beauties of the darks and grays. That the sun has been "hung" and the river "held" suggests that the things the speaker sees—the thin sun, the frozen river—are not accidents, but part of a composition meant to be witnessed, named, and appreciated. That the trees' bare branches can be seen as "black lace" suggests how the eye can reframe what is barren and see its beauty. The terms depend not only on the maker but on the viewer. And that the poem ends with the radiator that purrs "all day" offers a note of reassurance, but also a reminder of our vulnerable human condition. To appreciate the beauty and altered perspectives winter offers, we need that radiator to keep purring. It is the sound of safety. We depend on the utility company, on the infrastructure, on fuel production, on members of the communities we live in whose job it is to supply what we need. To behold the beauty of winter is a blessing. And a privilege.

Variable Grace

The tulip bulbs rest darkly in the fridge
To get the winter they can't get outside;
The drought and warm winds alter and abridge
The season till it almost seems denied.

A bright road-running scrub jay plies his bill,
While searching through the garden like a sleuth
For peanuts that he's buried in the soil:
How different from the winters of my youth.

Back in Vermont, we'd dress on furnace vents.
A breakfast of hot cereal—and then
We'd forge out to a climate so intense
It would have daunted Scott and Amundsen.

I'd race down icy Howard Street to catch
The school bus and pursue it, as it roared
Up Union, my arms waving, pleading, much
To the amusement of my friends on board.

But here I look out on a garden, whose
Poor flowers are knocked over on their side.
Well, stakes and ties will cure them of the blues
(If not the winds) and see them rectified.

And in the shower is a pail we use
To catch and save the water while it warms:
I fetch and pour it on the irises
And hope this winter will bring drenching storms.
                    —Timothy Steele, "December in Los Angeles"

Every December, the Christmas cards my mother displayed on the dining room sideboard tantalized me with images of snow, sleighs, icicles, and children wrapped in scarves and mittens. On cold days those Decembers, I'd take a jacket to school. Sometimes I'd button it up. Snow was something we might visit. We rarely had a chance to watch it fall.

Having grown up in Los Angeles County, I find the wistfulness in Steele's poem familiar. Living now in Northern California, where wildfires grow fiercer, more destructive, more unpredictable each year, and where extreme heat warnings last well into fall, I am led to reflect soberly on our experience of seasonality—how it organizes our deepest ideas of what is cyclical and stable, how it underlies and reinforces liturgical celebrations that mark the periods of feasting and fasting, repentance and celebration, by which so many have lived.

As icebergs melt and oceans warm and weather patterns shift, our sense of what we can count on is challenged in deep, disturbing ways. I think again of Auden's prophetic line, "Our sense of safety has to disappear." Curiously, some of that sense of safety has to do with the weather—a matter often relegated to the shallows of social chit-chat—a "safe" topic when politics or pandemic become too divisive.

But it's not safe at all, really: Weather connects us to everything—to the food system and infrastructures we rely on, to creatures who migrate, hibernate, swarm, burrow, and these days struggle to cope with threatened habitats and diminishing populations, to oceans and arid places, and to one another. Social patterns vary with the weather. What we see in the sky we recognize as harbinger.

What we see in the sky, as it lifts our gaze upward, may also lift up our hearts. Gray or lowering or dazzling blue, we still, on occasion, call the wide arc of sky "the heavens," and, when it darkens, may entertain fanciful thoughts, as Hopkins did, of "all the fire-folk sitting in the air." We may, in time of need or dread or ambient anxiety find our longing deepened for something beyond the confines of this fragile and ailing planet. In the very smallness of it, tucked into our corner of the Milky Way, we may take a certain ironic comfort: There is more. The universe is big. Creation is vast and various, and still "beautiful and new." We may be reminded, winter nights, that we are on a pilgrim journey and headed home where neither storms nor droughts will disturb us. Still wheeling through their cycles these planets and stars are only a few outward and visible signs of a singular, singing, immeasurable, and quite variable grace.

Mitigations

At four o'clock it's dark.
Today, looking out through dusk
at three gray women in stretch slacks
chatting in front of the post office,
their steps left and right and back
like some quick folk dance of kindness,
I remembered the winter we spent
crying in each other's laps.
What could you be thinking at this moment?
How lovely and strange the gangly spines
of trees against a thickening sky
as you drive from the library
humming off-key? Or are you smiling
at an idea met in a book
the way you smiled with your whole body
the first night we talked?
I was so sure my love of you was perfect,
and the light today
reminded me of the winter you drove home

each day in the dark at four o'clock
and would come into my study to kiss me
despite mistake after mistake after mistake.

—Michael Ryan, "In Winter"

They may offer us companionable "evenings under the lamplight," but long, dark winter evenings also open time for retrospection, memory, and perhaps regret as we look out through dusk at anonymous gray figures, and landscape turns into dreamscape. The "quick dance of kindness" among three chatting women on the sidewalk reawakens for the speaker in this poem his sorrow over what was lost "the winter we spent / crying in each other's laps."

Yet even as he is overtaken by a moment of mourning, the speaker begins to imagine the one he misses enjoying the "gangly" trees, smiling over an idea, driving home in this same evening, untroubled, humming, "off-key." Longing and sadness soften into something more generous as the "certain slant of light" on this winter afternoon uncovers another layer of memory: at just this time of day, before that winter of weeping, the beloved appeared in the study and greeted him with a kiss. Even present loneliness doesn't fully obscure the pleasure of those kisses, remembered.

We live with layers of memory whose shapes and colors mingle like a palimpsest. They inform and modify one another. Old offenses, suffered and committed, linger even after forgiveness has been offered and received, and cast their shadows over what comes after. We carry what has happened, and learn to bear it, to shoulder our stone sack of consequences even as we claim, if we are people whose worship includes weekly confession, the forgiveness and absolution that follow. The weight of regrets may lighten over time. The exonerating stories we weave about ourselves and our motives for our own comfort permit us to continue our bumpy journeys without debilitating guilt. But there will always be days when guilt resurfaces and an old litany sounds in the echo-chamber of memory reminding us of "mistake after mistake after mistake."

The word itself offers its own mitigation. Most of the wrongs we commit, when we see them as "mistakes," are committed in ignorance or misapprehension of where our good and our growth lie. It comes from an Old Norse word that means "miscarry." What was meant to live and flourish and take on its own life dies, sometimes by forces no one can trace. We speak of "miscarriages" of justice, remembering how many lives are altered by acts of jurisprudence gone awry. Our institutions—court, church, marriage—are meant to protect what we most cherish. Sometimes they don't. They, and we, make mistakes that alter lives forever.

Winter rememberings may be hard. In a season when the incidence of depression rises and loneliness is most acute, those of us who find ourselves lingering, lonely, at a window may need to weep again, even if there's no one in whose lap to weep. If we're among those who, untroubled for a time, find our way into shared spaces where we can enjoy a little dance of kindness, even with strangers in a bus queue or a checkout line, we might remember now and then to glance at the windows we pass, and nod to those who look out. Perhaps that is all it will take to remind them that a memory of kisses may be a harbinger of things to come.

Shades

Winter uses all the blues there are.
One shade of blue for water, one for ice,
Another blue for shadows over snow.
The clear or cloudy sky uses blue twice,
Both different blues. And hills row after row
Are colored blue according to how far.
You know the bluejay's double-blur device
Shows best when there are no green leaves to show.
And Sirius is a winterbluegreen star.
—Robert Francis, "Blue Winter"

In the opening chapter of Toni Morrison's *Beloved* an old woman in her final illness asks to see color—any color. It is winter and the Ohio landscape, what she can see of it from her window, is gray and white. "Since she knew death was anything but forgetfulness, she used the little energy left her for pondering color. 'Bring a little lavender in, if you got any. Pink, if you don't.'" Her need for color is a hunger that remains after food has lost its appeal. Her daughter brings what she can—"anything from fabric to her own tongue."

The muted colors of winter may make one long for the lush palette of summer but they retrain the eye to see lines and shapes in new terms—branches and garden tools and privet hedges buried in snow, darkened sky. Familiar scenes are estranged and made beautiful in new ways. And colors are newly noticeable and newly welcome—luxuries like jewels on gray days. The red of a cardinal in a snowy yard is a particular delight.

The inventory of blues in this small poem shows us a way of seeing worth emulating. The simple little verb "uses" assigns not only intention but artistic sensibility to winter. Like an artist with an array of shades at hand, winter has daubed blue everywhere, modulating it on different surfaces, as if to show how various and beautiful this one color can be—how each shade brings out something hidden behind the simple word, "blue." We learn to look and see more subtly as we adjust our gaze to landscapes where, even if snow doesn't lie on the ground, the vibrant colors of summer and fall have paled. When else would we be invited so explicitly to notice the several shades of brown or gray, or even shades of white?

Though scientists differ on the precise number depending on whether both chromaticity and luminosity are included, they seem to agree that the human eye can see 2.4 million colors. We are designed for levels of subtlety most of us rarely achieve—able to distinguish tones and weights and sizes as well as colors with remarkable nuance. From violinists to painters to botanists to physicians probing an abdomen for information, we recognize and measure excellence by that capacity for registering subtlety and receiving fine-tuned information. In *Moby-Dick*, Herman Melville's Ishmael muses, "Why then do you try to enlarge your mind? Subtilize it!" One way to consider our calling as beings who are "fearfully and wonderfully made" and exquisitely finely tuned is that: we are called to notice, and notice more, to distinguish and discern and imagine. Subtilizing our minds might make us more compassionate, less quick to judge, less inclined to dismiss, more careful about how we apply categories. Perhaps more intelligent in the broadest sense of that often misapplied word. Abraham Pais chose a title for his biography of Einstein he thought congruent to the scientist's own attitude toward the Creator: *Subtle Is the Lord*.

Traditional Montessori schools work to maintain the high standards Maria Montessori set for early childhood education. Her primary focus was to "educate the senses," believing, as St. Thomas Aquinas taught, that "All knowledge comes through the senses." To do that, weights and measures and bells and finely shaded chips of color are given to children to match by distinguishing minute differences between them. A child trained that way would have no problem imagining how many blues there are to see in a "blue winter." Or how many pinks in a sunset. Or how many ways white can look on a snowy morning.

Edna St. Vincent Millay's poem "Renascence" speaks of autumn woods that "all but cry with color." This poem speaks of a world not crying but whispering, perhaps: Look more closely. See what you see.

2

THE WILD IN WINTER

Our Common Home

The great sea stirs me.
The great sea sets me adrift,
It sways me like the weed
On a river-stone.

The sky's height stirs me.
The strong wind blows through my mind.
It carries me with it,
And moves my inner parts with joy.
—Uvavnuk, woman shaman of the Ingloolik Inuit

Let yourself be blessed. These words came to me, forcibly and almost audibly, in a particular moment of prayer years ago and have helped me stop my striving from time to time and open myself to blessing the way you open a curtain and light comes in. The curtain part is up to me.

There are other versions of this (I think divine) instruction: Let yourself be held. Let yourself be touched. Let yourself be changed.

The words of Uvavnuk, Ingloolik Inuit shaman, touch me. They bless me. Because she has let herself be blessed, awakened, stirred, set adrift, cleansed, and carried. The wisdom she imparts, it seems, is simply a testimony to what has happened to her: she has opened herself and been changed. Allowing herself to be moved by the sway of the sea, the spaciousness of the sky, the wind, she discovers a kind of joy that can't, finally, be imparted, but only acknowledged with gratitude.

Like heated glass, the forces that move through the grateful body are spun into words, translucent and inviting. This happened to me—a message whose other side is "This could happen to you." There are no imperatives here—only what Heschel called "radical amazement" at the deep simplicity of transformation.

And why are her words rendered as a poem—two spare stanzas? It may be a translator's choice, but if so, it's a good one. Each line ends at its own stopping point. We can rest there, taking the measure of how such things happen: how one may be stirred by the great sea—by its greatness, and by whatever in one's own body moves with its waves and deep currents. How one may recognize something of one's own life in the weed, tugged and held on stone, in water. How wind moves through our lungs, through the open spaces of the expectant heart, and lifts us into a new state—an altered state for which we have only the small word "joy."

The Inuit live in winter places. What they see around them is large. The light they live with comes and goes in long stretches—days and nights that might seem endless and daunting to us who live in more temperate latitudes. But perhaps their adaptation to long rhythms and more dramatic changes schools them in a habit of acceptance that prepares them for joy. When it comes in the morning, after a long, long night, making the wide sea visible once again, it fills the body and moves the "inner parts."

It matters to hear how those from other cultures than our own speak of joy—or sorrow or pain or healing. They can teach us more than we could know on our own about how to open our eyes and spirits wider to the gift of life on this earth, our common home.

Noticings

Dawn turned on her purple pillow,
And late, late came the winter day;
Snow was curved to the boughs of the willow,
The sunless world was white and grey.

At noon we heard a blue-jay scolding,
At five the last cold light was lost
From blackened windows faintly holding
The feathery filigree of frost.

—Sara Teasdale, "A December Day"

In a good poem, "simple description" isn't. Not simple at all. The precisions in these two elegant stanzas enable us to see what we couldn't without them. They awaken us not only to the beauty of a December day but to a way of seeing that day that will long outlast it. Turning on "her purple pillow" this dawn contrasts almost comically with Wordsworth's notion that "the mighty being is awake." Day comes reluctantly, and slowly. Snow clings and droops, and colors are muted. The day is marked by small, subtle things: shades of white and gray, the squawk of one bird, and finally, beautifully, a "feathery filigree of frost." It is all duly noted and noticed, and we are invited to notice, too, what, once noticed, is enhanced and made lovely like T. S. Eliot's roses that "had the look of flowers that are looked at."

Looking like this—appreciative, inventive, fanciful, and precise—is its own kind of prayer. The work of poetry is gratitude. Also rhyme, alliteration and assonance, personification and precise word choices. Blue jays do scold. Frost on glass is feathery. And at five, in midwinter, light is "lost." Suddenly, unlike lazy dawn, dark comes and a "sunless" day is completed.

The best poems and the best prayers are specific. They begin with noticings. They focus sharply on what has been closely noticed. A limited palette intensifies rather than diminishing what it is possible to see: white and gray, the small signifiers of passing time, the curve on one branch or one temporary lightfall can become breathtaking. Then we breathe again and look for words to mark the place where it happened.

Winter is a season of subtleties, unlike autumn, for instance, with woods that, in Millay's words, "all but cry with color." Being required to see more subtly, look more closely, revises our blunted sense of what is remarkable, and matters. It changes the dimensions of the days and moments habit has flattened into apparent uniformity and can train us to look again where there seemed nothing more to see.

It's good training. There's always something more. Looking around at more urban winter landscapes, we may have allowed ourselves to stop noticing who is unsheltered, who is shivering, carrying groceries in thin shirtsleeves, or, looking upward, to notice faint rainbows in passing clouds, the shine of steeple tops in pale sunlight, how rain darkens a maple's bark. It's all of a piece: noticing the quiet shifting of the natural world, noticing the look in neighbors' eyes, noticing the animals and plants that care for us as we care for them. Noticing keeps us connected to our fellow creatures—all of them, great and small—even the least conspicuous—and helps us find our place, humbly and joyfully, among them.

Midwinter Moonlight

How thin and sharp is the moon tonight!
How thin and sharp and ghostly white
Is the slim curved crook of the moon tonight!
               —Langston Hughes, "Winter Moon"

Small poems may invite us to large thoughts, but only by way of a narrow passage—here consisting of three lines—two exclamatory sentences that might seem simply redundant if one didn't pause for a second look.

Like Japanese haiku, this tiny poem by a great urban poet of the Harlem Renaissance might easily be glanced at, passed by, and forgotten, but for something peculiarly arresting that tugs at our own memories of midwinter moonlight. It is an observation many of us have made on evening walks in winter when the night sky comes into sharp focus in the cold. The midwinter light is sparse but striking in chill air that reminds us, on the coldest nights, what a thin zone of life-supporting warmth we inhabit. We live on a precarious riparian edge between earth and heaven.

Thin and *sharp* seem at first glance like simple descriptors, but they are not inviting words, nor are *ghostly* or *crook*. The lines are resonant with something unsettling and unnamed—a sense of danger or threat from just beyond this world. Sometimes, of course, when we look at the moon, we enjoy its familiarity and beauty. We have watched it wax and wane throughout the seasons of our lives. Some of us track its phases and with them the subtle rhythms of lives too much constrained by calendar time. We imagine "her" as a feminine being or "him" as an old man gazing benevolently from afar. Huge orange harvest moons are thrilling and somehow reassuring—wide and warm and radiant.

But the thin, sharp, ghostly, crooked moon of this night is a reminder of mortality and darkness. Our vulnerability, suddenly remembered, takes us by surprise. We can forget, in a day, that we are not altogether in charge of our choices, our fortunes, our span on this planet. We can forget we are on a planet; focused on the immediacies of being in a house, an office, on a piece of land that is "ours" as we put it. But the night sky reminds us that we are earthlings—that the boundaries we draw are meaningless against the vast backdrop of the universe, and that we have our being in the invisible, immortal presence of a Creator who holds "our times" in great, mysterious hands.

For some, those times are indeed precarious. Langston Hughes wrote this poem in 1923. Jim Crow laws were in full force. Even life in Harlem, where a lively culture of poetry and jazz was emerging among Black Americans, "night life" was not safe. Hard things happened under the thin, sharp moon. To read the poem now is to be reminded of the chronic apprehension many live with still.

But the poem offers more than that an unsettling glimpse of vulnerability. Even though "Winter Moon" is a mere three lines, it represents a sustained gaze—looking and looking again, seeing and inferring a bit more on second glance. Years ago, a practitioner I saw for acupuncture and other treatments offered me a startling prescription: "Go out every night," he said, "and gaze at the moon for two full minutes." He didn't explain himself. I followed his prescription—not faithfully every night, I admit, but on the nights I betook myself to the balcony and gazed dutifully at the moon, I received something back. I couldn't quite identify what it was— peace? A sense of my own smallness and the smallness of our little planet? A dizzying sense of the "faraway nearby"? All of these, perhaps, and also an inducement to pray, or at least to remember the Psalmist's prayer: "When I consider thy heavens, the work of thy fingers, the moon and the stars, which thou hast ordained, What is man, that thou art mindful of him?" (Psalm 8:4). I cite the lines from the King James version, since that is how I learned them as a child. Even without the more gender-inclusive language of newer versions, I feel included in the awe that has informed many generations of sky-gazers before mine.

There is awe in "Winter Moon," as well, and wonder at the tiny glimpse we get every night of a heavenly body that is both "ours" and alien—a nightly mystery hanging in a sky under which, however troubled, we live and move and play out our stories together.

Inscriptions

The backyard is one white sheet
Where we read in the bird tracks

The songs we hear. Delicate
Sparrow, heavier cardinal,

Filigree threads of chickadee.
And wing patterns where one flew

Low, then up and away, gone
To the woods but calling out

Clearly its bright epigrams.
More snow promised for tonight.

The postal van is stalled
In the road again, the mail

Will be late and any good news
Will reach us by hand.

—Nancy McCleery, "December Notes"

One of the earliest surviving examples of musical notation comes from 1400 BCE in Babylonia. The figures seem to represent marks on lyre strings. They look very like bird tracks. Early alphabets also look, to the untrained eye, a little like scratchings in snow. Learning how to render what we hear, see, feel, or imagine in writing has involved many human efforts to capture, distill, and translate what defies all those efforts—the numinous, fleeting, pulsing breath of being—into inscriptions. All our alphabets are vestiges. Written poems, like sheet music, are precious records which, however, do not fully live until they are spoken or sung.

It is why we still gather, when we can, to hear sacred words read, to sing, to converse, to breathe life into all that comes to us mediated and modified. We are surrounded by inscriptions left by what has been and gone. In such a world, media-saturated, we express our longing for immediacy in cries of delight when we are surprised by life in its swift and glittering forms: Look! A hummingbird! A dragonfly! A doe and her fawn! These small encounters are sometimes no more than a momentary impression of what has already disappeared, but they leave us with something subtler than birdsong, each its own testimony to "news" that keeps happening, and, despite predation and the privations of winter, is good.

Mary Oliver's poem, "Mozart, for Example," calls similar attention to how birds who bring us "all the quick notes / Mozart didn't have time to use" model a persistent happiness that survives even the darkest days. We need their messages, and each other's, whether in indecipherable song or in—"bright epigrams" as McCleery calls them—a form of statement that is pithy, clever, often comic, always surprising. We need their innocent gospel now, perhaps, more than ever, in the very midst of lament that a third of their number have disappeared as habitats dwindle, that Hopkins's insistence that "nature is never spent" may have been premature. We need it, this poet suggests, more than we need the morning mail or the evening news.

Hundreds of times in scripture we are reminded to "listen" or to "hear." The history of the word "listen" in English links it to "obey." Listening, attention, pausing, noticing, appreciating are all forms of obedience. Really to listen is to accept an invitation on the terms in which it's given, to lay aside distraction and redirect our energies. I like what happens to the word when I link it to prepositions: listen into, listen with, listen beyond, listen behind—more deeply, remembering and recognizing echoes of what I've heard before.

Living in Light

The morning when I first notice
the leaves starting to color,
early orange, and back-lit,
I think how rapture doesn't
vanish, merely fades into
the background, waits for those
moments between moments.

I think this and the door opens,
the street takes on its glistening
look, Bay fog lifting, patches of sun
on sycamore—yellow sea.
I am in again, and swimming.

—Alice Jones, "Light"

Accounts of near-death experiences tell of entering the light—
not just seeing it, but being in it, as in water—a luminous,

encompassing fluidity. The ambient light is not just brilliant, but rapturous. Even on this darkened planet, we dwell in it. We swim in it. Now and then we notice it.

Though Alice Jones's poem speaks of light in early fall, I include it here because in this season when Jews celebrate a "feast of lights" and Christians sing about the Light shining in the darkness, light deserves renewed reflection. The way we live by it and in it. The way it leads us to paradox—wave and particle—and connects us with the trillion points of light in dark space that make up "our" galaxy.

The speaker in the poem identifies a moment of noticing that comes "between moments." That in-between place is where epiphany happens. Suddenly a stray thought interrupts our puzzlings and dispels confusion, or a remembered image appears as in a dream and we are moved by a wave of feeling we can't quite explain. Or a hummingbird hovers and seems to bring a personal greeting from beings of other orders—and we are reassured, though we don't know quite why. These moments are precious, and unpredictable. We can't make them happen, though some claim that the more we notice them, the more they come. They are little reminders of how things really are—brighter, subtler, more exquisite than we tend to recognize as we walk around on Middle Earth, gazing into middle space, largely unamazed.

Abraham Heschel's term "radical amazement," which he identifies as the state in which the wisest among us live, comes to mind as I imagine the "glistening look" of a street, sun in sycamores, and a yellow sea. I imagine a way to cultivate radical amazement as a habit of mind might be simply to say to oneself,

"Oh, look!" The way Gerard Manley Hopkins said to himself on some night walk through Oxford, "Look at the stars! Look, look up at the skies! / O look at all the firefolk sitting in the air!" A more advanced practice might be then to say, "Wait! Look again!" Because seeing comes in layers—the street, the fog, the sycamores one by one.

As seeing unfurls into more seeing, we may find ourselves rapt—enraptured—by the sudden sense that every growing thing in sight looks a little more alive, and its claim on our attention is a little stronger. "Rapture" is a term that may need to be reclaimed from Victorian novels and from noisy, churchy debates about apocalypse. In medieval Latin its common meaning was to be "carried off, seized, abducted." Only later, around 1600, was it appropriated as a way of describing spiritual ecstasy or an altered, "higher" state of awareness. I like knowing of its rather violent origins, as I like John Donne's edgy sonnet, "Batter my heart" where he insists that if we are to be reclaimed from sloth and spiritual squalor, we will have to be seized, snatched, overcome by a Love that breaks all barriers to reach us.

It does. It opens a chasm, and we fall in. Or lifts the veil and we peek through. It flickers and goes. It is momentary, mysterious, and baffling. And utterly steadfast.

Happenings

Outside
tuned in to the night-blooming cereus
channel 1 a.m.

Creamy petals
halfway open
striking white
when a crack of thunder
split the sky
ruffling branches
gust of cold

It was winter in a minute
O I could miss who said what said
but catch the coming of winter
let me be there
please
   —Naomi Shihab Nye, "What News Are You Listening To?"

When does the change take place? We ask this with wonder when we look at children who have suddenly, subtly, inexplicably become adolescents, apparently overnight. We ask it as we notice how long it's been since putting weight on a certain joint has been uncomfortable, or when we notice a scar has diminished to invisibility, or anxiety has melted into acceptance. The question hovers in the air as seasons change. Anything can be a benchmark: a leaf falling, a coat grabbed from the closet after months of disuse, morning dark over the hills where only last week the sun rose in time for morning coffee.

In this poem by a poet who has lived much of her life in the warm weather of Texas, the night-blooming cereus is one of those markers that tell us what time it is. Cereus is a cactus flower that blooms only at night. Its exquisite densely petaled blooms don't last long, but they're worth getting up to see, like shooting stars or a lunar eclipse. Even as the speaker watches this little luminous happening under the night sky, winter comes. Thunder, wind, and a chill announce what has gathered and crested and now—just at one a.m., just as the cereus opens—and the speaker, catching her breath, I imagine, finds herself present to witness that mysterious moment. This, she thinks, is when it happened: winter came "in a minute," and she was there to watch.

I remember lying on a hillside with my daughters near a campsite in August, watching for shooting stars. Every few minutes a streak of light would cross the sky among the many tiny flickerings. You couldn't anticipate when it would happen or in which part of the sky; you had to let your vision go soft and scan the whole dome of night while you waited. You could miss it if you looked away. You wanted to stay awake and catch just that moment. Each shooting star came and went quickly but left a little thrill of wonder and pleasure.

These are things that don't make the news—the little happenings that leave traces invisible to the naked eye. Any one of them—a crack of thunder, a chill wind, a sound in the trees—may announce the change of season. The speaker is there to witness the coming of winter. Thoreau, whose prophetic warnings to an industrializing age included strong words about the distractions of what passed for "news" in Boston tabloids, made the point in *Walden* that the speaker in this poem so simply and elegantly reiterates in the final lines: what is always new, and the "news" we would most benefit from noticing, is the small, subtle, surprising events taking place in the natural world around us. Everywhere in the created order, from wheeling galaxies to shifting tectonic plates to unfolding flowers, all things are being "made new." Annie Dillard's comment on the many constant amazements taking place on the banks of Tinker Creek was similar to Thoreau's and to Nye's: "the least we can do is show up." And perhaps occasionally, pray the prayer this poet offers us: "Let me be there / please."

Into the Depths

Clouds like white knuckles gather at the horizon and stop.
The air is thin with heat; we move through it quickly,
our fingers making short, uncontrollable gestures,
signals out of the mouth of our hands, which we cup
and hold before us not in prayer, but in the hope
that an empty hand will be filled, that our desires
are obvious and real, like our love of rain.

—Gary Young, "Winter Drought"

In an online meeting, speaking from California with folks in Michigan, I shamelessly expressed my complete lack of sympathy with their complaints about the cold, rainy weather and snow. Out here where wildfires have devastated millions of exquisite acres and demolished homes over the past several "fire seasons" and parched leaves blow in dry wind, we pray for rain. If there were a local rain dance happening, I'd go with my drum.

Gary Young's "Winter Drought" offers a sobering but refreshingly authentic counterpoint to what have become incessant December songs about chestnuts roasting and letting it snow. Tinny versions of those standards, interspersed with invitations to deck the halls and dream by the fire, continue, even in a year of record heat and climate disasters, to be piped through sound systems in stores we can't seem to entirely avoid.

There's nothing wrong with good cheer, of course. Certainly nothing wrong with the real hope and reflection and spiritual renewal so many manage to find in this season despite the noise and tinsel. But in a difficult season of disease and disruption, as the news cycle reels from crisis to crisis, it's essential to resist pretense. If there's hope or faith or joy to proclaim to the world, it has to come from the deepest places—deeper than the profound discouragements we face in public life, and the daily reality of our own and others' sorrows.

What draws me back to "Winter Drought" is not only its apt description of a state of mind and body drought brings on—apprehension, anxiety, watchful awareness of a mortal need—but also the prayer it describes at the end. The speaker holds out hope (which he resists even calling prayer) "that an empty hand will be filled," a cupped palm waiting for water that is nowhere to be found. But the second prayer seems to come from an even deeper place of need: "that our desires are obvious and real, like our love of rain."

Reading his poem, I think of the needs of those whose situations most of us can barely imagine: political refugees; people in squalid detention centers, separated from their children; families living in buildings drones have struck or where occupiers' bulldozers have razed their homes; people dying from contaminated water, or of thirst. Their desires are obvious and real. They need to eat and drink that which is not contaminated. They need their children, who need them. They need to be safe and work and live. Sensationalizing their plight or minimizing it or simply politicizing it offends good taste and charity. The only honorable response is to see the need, name it, and participate in some way in meeting it or, since we can't send rain, entering into deeper solidarity with those who suffer most, letting our love of them be like our love of rain: full of longing that half-measures can't assuage.

Holy Ground

It is as if the light that is to come
had taken on a flake-like form and substance
laid itself, in silhouette, along, against,
the windward part
of every naked trunk and branch.
The ground below lies cloaked,
each blade of grass or bracken
with its glistening garment,
so that, even at the darkest hour last night,
a luminescence shone as if reflected
from whatever burns within.
Might the bright, promised realm
lie here and now revealed,
its last impediment
my faltering fear to enter in?

—J. Barrie Shepherd, "Forest Snowfall"

"Light from light," a phrase that summons the mind toward
mystery, is one of the loveliest liturgical descriptions of Christ. It

echoes the poetic image of God "clothed in light as in a garment." And the astonished, grateful awareness of the Psalmist's epiphany: "In your light do we see light" (Psalm 36:9). "God is light," we read in 1 John (1 John 1:5). Sometimes, in a moment like this one in "forest snowfall" just before dawn, trees, too, and grass blades are clothed in light.

The first sentence of this poem invites us to recognize in winter moonlight not only a harbinger of dawn, but the real presence of "the light that is to come." What we await is already here, moving among us, falling upon us like a blessing. Or it shines forth from every living being, and even from those we dully think "inanimate." Energy gathers into form. It draws and holds our gaze. It draws and holds us.

I recently heard a story about a near-death experience in which a woman, having left her body, saw, as many have reported in similar accounts, what was happening in the room where her body lay "dead." What was distinctive about this story was not just that the part of her that was very much alive hovered and witnessed the moment from just outside the physical realm, but that she saw each person in the room swathed in a kind of energetic "mantle" that seemed to make their emotional energy visible to her. Like the ground in this poem that lies "cloaked"—"each blade of grass or bracken / with its glistening garment," reflecting "whatever burns within"—it seems to me entirely possible that we, too, wear garments of light, though visible only to the occasional eyes that see.

Near-death stories abound at this point, perhaps because they have become a slightly more respectable focus of scientific scrutiny, and perhaps also because more people are successfully resuscitated and return from a place just beyond the domain of this life. Or perhaps they are receiving more attention because our hunger for assurance of life after life has grown apace as we face increasingly dire possibilities of global catastrophe. What is common to those stories is the light—being drawn to it, drawn into it, warmed and welcomed by it, experiencing it as love energy. God is light. God is love. Somehow many of these stories reaffirm those twin claims.

Poets who dwell and ponder and walk solitary in woods, sometimes at night, see it, too—light glistening on leaves, playing on the surface of a pond, or on, or in, snow-covered ground. Epiphany lies all around us, if we pause. The two "as ifs" in the first stanza of "Forest Snowfall" open a door of possibility: maybe what we see is luminescent, not just reflective; maybe this bush is a burning bush. And the "maybe" that begins the second stanza pushes the door a little wider open as the poet, beginning with what is carefully hypothetical, edges toward the kind of consent Moses must have given when he heard the voice of God and took off his shoes to stand on what he suddenly saw was holy ground.

Past into Present

Behind the glass, I hear
the muted cries of grosbeaks
finding winter berries.
The year's darkest day
is almost past; a thin
rain falls, and yet the meager
winter bush is fruited
with birds, even as summer
nested them among
its leaves. Let the window
darken; I will not see
them fly away, but turn
my thoughts to the inside weather.
I will see, in firelight, summer
shapes like theirs, but not
their abundant mime on the bare
boughs. Let the dead wood
wholly bloom with flame;
strike the match; let the paper

> flare with a yellow cry.
> Half a year or half a world
> away, some birds kindle
> green evening trees at solstice.
>
> —Gene Baro, "Mid-Winter"

One thing replaces another. And each thing is irreplaceable. As this poem moves our attention from outdoors to indoors, birds become fruit and their wings tongues of fire. We begin to see how each thing in the created world points to and displaces others in a seasonal dance of difference and resemblance and, by the magic of metaphor, becomes those others.

Seasons interpenetrate in memory: a winter fire recalls the "summer shapes" of birds, sharp wings spread. Then the dead wood blooms with flame, then glares "with a yellow cry." The distinctions we draw between animate and inanimate blur as we look. The long gaze at a flickering fire invites us into dreamspace that lies just outside time. Summer is not lost—only in another place where birds "kindle" green evening trees even now.

"We had the experience," T. S. Eliot writes, "but missed the meaning. Approach to the meaning restores the experience in a different form." In winter, this poem reminds us, summer comes back to us as an image and a memory, a persisting dimension of what has displaced it—the cold, the dark days, the bare branches. We live among vestiges of the past. It surfaces in the present like an image painted over, changing the tone of the lived moment.

When I discovered the liturgical year as an adult, I found myself fascinated by the way the distinctive seasons—Advent, Christmastide, Lent, Eastertide, Pentecost, and the long season of "ordinary time"—invited us to a particular part of the great biblical story, but also echoed and mirrored the others and reminded us that "all is always now." Traditionally, Advent is a "little Lent," a time of fasting and praying and waiting. And the coming of the Holy Spirit at Pentecost brings with it a memory of the burning bush and Babel, and of the messenger of God whose word awakened "the handmaid of the Lord," and what was done unto her began its long, consequential unfolding. No season is simply what it is: childhood brings foreshadowing of what may come to be and old age memories not only of what has been, but of what might have been. In our dreams, in sudden scraps of conversation overheard or a few measures of music, we discover just under the surface of consciousness what has been there all along. It's all here.

"Nothing is lost," Cowper writes, "but may be found, if sought." It is the seeking eye that finds surprise or message or reminder or invitation wherever the eye alights. When we see that way, as the speaker does here, blessing is received and imparted. The green of summer comes vividly to mind in midwinter, and firelight is full of birds' wings and, in its own miraculous way, dead wood blooms.

Other Beings

A little heat in the iron radiator,
the dog breathing at the foot of the bed,

and the windows shut tight,
encrusted with hexagons of frost.

I can barely hear the geese
complaining in the vast sky,

flying over the living and the dead,
schools and prisons, and the whitened fields.
—Billy Collins, "Winter"

We need the wild geese. We need to witness the lives of nonhuman creatures to take the measure of our own—our vulnerabilities to the elements and the seasons, our presumptions, our false securities. The call of the wild geese is a reminder to the speaker in this poem, and through him, to us, to lift our hearts and our gaze and our imaginations to a world wider than the small, warm circles of security we draw tight around ourselves in winter.

We need reminders of the wild. We need them more the less wild we become. Thoreau's insistence that "in wildness is the preservation of the world" is not only a call for deeper attention to care for wild spaces and creatures but also to awareness of our own dependence on the processes, the ecosystems, the habits, and the knowledge of beings who sometimes become our food but perhaps more often, just outside the radius of our limited attention, preserve what we need. They transport seeds; they fertilize soil; they consume harmful insects; they sustain the gift cycles that sustain life on earth. They are members of the beloved communities we belong to. They are our neighbors.

The last two lines of this simple poem are haunting. The living and the dead, those in schools and those in prisons, and all the spaces we have "plotted and pieced" into property lie equally under their purview. They pass over them, and they are gone. They must be "about their Father's business," indifferent to ours, though intimately connected with it. We, meanwhile, turn up the heat and stroke the sleeping dog.

"Meanwhile" is a valuable word. It helps us reset—not get so entangled in our own immediacies and anxieties that we forget the parallel lives and other stories happening all around us. We settle behind closed windows with a book. Meanwhile the migration patterns of geese and butterflies, the swarming of bees, the foraging of polar bears on diminishing ice fields are shifting slightly. From where they see it, the world looks threateningly rectangular. The currents of air and water that offer them guidance are warming and changing. They adapt, little by little, to our incursions and develop new strategies. Deer descend from hillside habitats to find water in suburbs. Rabbits burrow in new places as bulldozers clear their meadows. Species seek new habitats. Some die out. Viruses are released into new hosts. We are all surviving, some of us thriving, amid crosscurrents we can't fully map or account for, though we need those who try. Meanwhile we can, occasionally, listen to the wild geese and, imagining the world they see, widen our frames of reference, adjust our hopes, and consider what is happening, meanwhile, in places where it is, even now, summer.

What the Trees Relinquish

All the complicated details
of the attiring and
the dis-attiring are completed!
A liquid moon
moves gently among
the long branches.
Thus having prepared their buds
against a sure winter
the wise trees
stand sleeping in the cold.

—William Carlos Williams, "Winter Trees"

This poem, like so many Williams, doctor and poet, wrote on prescription pads late at night after making his rounds among the poor, shares a certain whimsical sensibility with the haiku poets. It falls into three separable parts. The first recalls the annual cycle of a deciduous tree's life, leafing and unleafing, with the personifying and slightly suggestive verbs "attiring and dis-attiring." The process involves "complicated details"—an observation a male of his generation might have made amusedly about the mysteries of a woman's rituals of dressing and undressing. It is also botanically accurate. From budding to falling, leaves are formed from soil, sunlight, and water. Special cells ferry nutrients to the budding sites. A great deal of work goes on under the surface for a tree to produce its particular beauty and shade, all of it intricately interdependent. The whole of it dependent on climate and the community of neighboring trees. The exclamation point at the end of the first three lines of Williams's poem, uncharacteristic for a poet often wry and understated, is well deserved.

From the windows of squalid tenements where he made house calls, Williams's eyes must have found respite in trees, even the bare ones, especially on winter nights when, waiting through a woman's prolonged labor or keeping death-watch with a patient, he saw the "liquid moon" moving among long, bare branches. Again, the lines echo the long, rich Japanese haiku tradition of attention to the moon—its beauty, its evocativeness, the subtle way it reminds us of time that is not clock time, how things change in its reflected light. In an earlier chapter, I mentioned a practitioner I consulted who suggested that I step outside every night and spend two minutes gazing at the moon. It was a calming practice, and reorienting after a day's distractions. It was quieting and humbling and somehow reassuring. It took me back to lines from psalms I learned as a child (hence the King James version—standard reading in our family): "When I consider thy heavens, the work of thy fingers, the moon and the stars, which thou hast ordained, what is man, that thou art mindful of him? and the son of man, that thou visitest him?" (Psalm 8:4). The speaker in Williams's poem considers the heavens and sees a "liquid" and "gentle" moon—words that speak of flow and presence. That the moon moves "among" the branches flattens geophysical space into a kind of dreamscape or symbolic space of the kind we see in medieval paintings, where the perspective of the human eye gives way to the always-here-and-now representation of what is eternally present from the perspective of faith. The moon and the tree and the witnessing mind are brought into intimate relation for a moment of seeing something true that may only be visible when factuality gives way to a unifying, poetic vision of what is.

The third section of the poem begins with "Thus," leading us to see what is presented in the first two as preparatory: the yearly round of arboreal tasks is completed, the trees stand, receptive, bathed in moonlight, and all is made ready, protected and sealed against the coming cold. So now the wise trees can sleep. Some cultures recognize trees as wise ones—elders and neighbors. Botanist writer Robin Wall Kimmerer reminds her readers that her Indigenous people recognize trees, along with other nonhuman species, as neighbors, givers, protectors. Other botanists have written recently about the "hidden life" of trees, about the ways they care for their neighbors and their young, about the ways they communicate danger and adapt to it. The wisdom of trees is not mere poetic fancy. To think of them as our neighbors is to open ourselves to a layer of awareness, reverence, and even awe, and perhaps to a renewed sense of mutual responsibility and reciprocity. In the poem, the wisdom of trees lies not only in the way they prepare themselves and protect their buds for the cold of winter, but in their sleeping. We are reminded, finally, that one measure of wisdom lies in relinquishing control and acquiescing to one of the fundamental conditions of living: We need rest. We need sleep. Every creature needs, daily, to entrust the vulnerable self to the care of others and of the protective, sustaining Spirit that breathes in us even in our deepest slumber. In that letting go lies the form of wisdom we call trust—not just a virtue, but a condition of survival.

Invitations

Winter solitude—
in a world of one color
the sound of wind. (33)

　Winter garden,
　the moon thinned to a thread,
　insects singing. (44)

　　First winter rain—
　　even the monkey
　　seems to want a raincoat. (28)

When the winter chrysanthemums go,
there's nothing to write about
but radishes.

　　　　　　　　　　—Matsuo Basho, Four Haiku

Most traditional haiku make reference to seasons. All we do takes
place in a seasonal context. Single moments of awareness emerge

in the light and wind and rhythms of early spring or late fall or the deep chill of winter. Like the wide spaces in which a single strike on a brass bowl may resonate, haiku work concentrically, offering the reader a moment of surprise that ripples outward into memory and hope and desire, often mixing levity with longing. They remind us that surprise lurks in the most ordinary objects and small events. They remind us that we live in relation to other orders of being—to moon and wind and animals and insects. They remind us that laughter lurks at the edges even of apprehension or loss—that emotions, like colors and seasons, bleed into each other and sometimes pool and eddy in surprising places.

These winter haiku invite us to imagine our way into a moment in the wide context of a winter season and imagine our way into a place that is both utterly particular and common as soil and wind. We live in paradox. We live in multiple frames, they insist. Vitality and resilience and ultimately wisdom depend on the agility with which we can switch frames and hold the awareness that comes from peering closely as we rise and widen our gaze to include the moon and feel the embrace of the passing wind.

In the first of these four, a "world of one color" offers little that surprises the eye of the lone looker. Landscape seems flattened and reduced. The phrase itself suggests language I've heard people use to describe periods of depression: colorless, gray, blank. Then our attention is turned to the wind. The sudden switch from one sense experience to another is also a switch from noun to verb, and from what seems to lack vibrancy to ambient vibration. Even as we may seem to be surrounded by dormancy and death, a reminder of life energy moves all around us. As so many who have lost their sight have testified, when one sense is muted or lost another may compensate, new kinds of attentiveness become possible, and with them new information. They learn a way to receive the world on different terms. Subtly, as the seasons change, so do we.

The second of these haiku situates the speaker (and us) in a winter garden—a place where most growth, if it is happening, takes place underground—root vegetables and bulbs hibernate out of sight. And as there is little visible flourishing, little left of summer's abundance, so there is little light from a moon "thinned to a thread." Whatever one may have seen by its light is dimmed now. But again, what is lost to the eye is offered to the ear. Insects sing into the darkness. The speaker hears in the sound something more than chirp or buzz: every creature, if you listen, he implies, has its song. The little poem, if it does its work, leaves us with questions to carry into our own long winter evenings: What sings? If I listen, whose song might I hear? And might it just be that the choir or sounds from nonhuman beings is a gift, freely given or, possibly, an invitation to sing along?

Listening to other beings awakens and widens our sympathies— a thought the third haiku amplifies in the image of a drenched and shivering monkey. In the "first winter rain" everyone under the overcast sky is gathered into the moment of transition. We all need new layers of protection: autumn's relief from blazing heat has chilled into wind and rain. The title of a book I read years ago comes to mind as I pause over this poem: Marjorie Dorner's *Seasons of Sun and Rain*. It traces the evolving responses of five women just beyond mid-life, deeply bonded in long-term friendship, to a sixth friend's descent into dementia. They vary from denial to heartache to anger to acceptance and finally to imaginative strategies of adaptation. The way haiku calls our attention to seasonality seems to me a gentle, insistent reminder that the shifts and changes we encounter from one time or year to the next are an invitation to life: to be lively in its deepest sense is to be adaptive and imaginative. In the moment when the speaker in this third poem notices the monkey, something new happens: he sees this little fellow being on new terms and—no doubt smiling—imagines him needing what humans need. Of course he doesn't; he will do what monkeys do to find protection, and that, too, awakens awareness. We are vulnerable in our own peculiarly human ways. It's good to be humble about that.

The last of these winter poems seems to me the most playful, though by definition haiku are playful. It takes us from a rather abject and bedraggled image of loss and death—winter chrysanthemums dried and brown and perhaps cloaked in frost—to the cheery, plump, ruddy, hearty, dirty image of a radish. Where the more delicate delights diminish, something sturdy and resilient might become apparent.

But the poem does one more thing: it's a poem about the speaker, and about the speaker as a writer looking for an object of attention on which to wreak his gifts. "What is there to write about?" is not an unfamiliar question for writers wondering where to go next with their trove of words and the open page before them. We don't always have to write of what is high-minded or even beautiful, the poet seems to say. Sometimes what is given for our learning is something as unpoetic and unpromising as a radish. What will make the radish an object of interest, if not a thing of beauty, is the quality of attention we bring to it. Whatever the eye falls upon is an invitation: Look. See. Notice! And then, it may be, you might eat the radish and find it surprisingly delicious.

3

SOUL WORK IN WINTER

Beyond Safety

Out of a silence greater than all words;
Over the unspeakable, dumb,
Everlasting hills
With their muter herds;
Swifter than a blade that kills;
Mightier than prayer;
Fairer than the dawn
When some dew yet remains unbroken;
Stronger than despair;
From the unspoken to the spoken,
While the heart rests momently;
Lovely as the half-uttered words of a child,
More delicate, more mild;
Terrible as the torn breasts of anguish
When strong wills languish:
Suddenly, dreadfully, exquisitely,
Love, death, and God shall come.

—Charles Murphy, "Advent"

Advent is a necessary season: those who pray to live by holy guidance have to reckon, in this season of bleak landscapes and threatening weather, with the birth of what Yeats called "a terrible beauty." Paradox permeates all sacred traditions. What we most long for can be reached, they teach, only by walking through our greatest fears. And the love that reaches out to us from "out of that silence greater than all words" is, T. S. Eliot reminds us, the same love "that wove / the intolerable shirt of flame." The story that culminates in Christmas begins with the "threefold terror of love" Yeats described in a poem that hovers as a backdrop to this one:

> . . . a fallen flare
> Through the hollow of an ear;
> Wings beating about the room;
> The terror of all terrors that I bore
> The Heavens in my womb.
>
> ("The Mother of God")

From conception to birth it is a story of unfolding, ongoing mystery, fraught with risk and political threat and disrupted expectations. Hope, it teaches us, is not the same as expectation, but often rather the opposite—the kind of hope Eliot wrote about when he admonished us to "wait without hope, for hope would be hope for the wrong thing."

The period of waiting churches have associated with Advent is a reenactment of the anticipation those astonished human players felt as they took their humble parts in a divine drama. It is also a reminder of the promise of the "new heaven and new earth" for which we wait, and of our own deaths and what comes after. It is a period when Christians are called to listen beyond the ambient cultural noise to what can only be heard in silence. "Still, still, still," an old carol begins. The holy night is a silent night.

The descriptors that line Murphy's litany of Advent hope are not altogether comforting words: unspeakable, swifter, mightier, fairer, stronger, terrible. Whatever comes toward us will take us by divine surprise. We are as defenseless against the moment of epiphany and the summons it brings as against the "blade that kills." I know from sitting with the dying as a hospice volunteer how even the gentlest death is shocking in the chasm it opens between what we call life and what we call death. I also know, having witnessed both, how right Eliot's magi were about the similarities between our coming hence and our going hither: both involve rupture. "I had seen birth and death," one of them says, "but I thought they were different."

The poem's final paradoxical assurance, "Love, death, and God shall come," suggests obliquely that the Holy Spirit, the promised Comforter, might well be mistaken for the Angel of Death. Advent takes us to the outer edge of safety to a place beyond all we can try to make safe, and leads us to relinquish our dream of safety for an awakening far more lasting and costly and full of unsought, surprising joy.

Ancient Assurances

There was a church in Umbria, Little Portion,
Already old eight hundred years ago.
It was abandoned and in disrepair
But it was called St. Mary of the Angels
For it was known to be the haunt of angels,
Often at night the country people
Could hear them singing there.

What was it like, to listen to the angels,
To hear those mountain-fresh, those simple voices
Poured out on the bare stones of Little Portion
In hymns of joy?
No one has told us.
Perhaps it needs another language
That we have still to learn,
An altogether different language.
             —Anne Porter, "An Altogether Different Language"

I know people who have had visions and heard voices—modern mystics, otherwise perfectly ordinary people, who seemed simply to hear or see a little further out on the spectrum than most of us. I know people who notice the vibrations of things, who pick up signals, whose awareness includes subtleties most of us miss. I know people who know better than most that trees are living beings, that bee colonies and flocks of birds share a singlemindedness humans seem to have forgotten or foregone. I know people who have come back from near-death changed. I know people who have traveled to "thin" places where the veil between this dimension and the next becomes more permeable and translucent. And I wonder, as this poet does, what it takes to reach our listening a little further and hear angels.

Perhaps hearing those songs does require an "altogether different language." But my guess is that the country people of Umbria and the shepherds on ancient Middle Eastern hillsides and the many since who have heard song in silence or seen figures in light have had access to the divine not because of extraordinary gifts or practices but because they have not lost or squandered or overridden or repressed what most of us smother with a blanket of rationality that seems to keep us secure.

Prayer is a language. You learn it, I sometimes think, by letting go, gradually, of words, or making more spaces between them where the voice of God can be heard. Contemplative practices like centering prayer or breath prayer or quiet meditation open avenues of grace along which those less visible and audible to human ears may travel to meet us, and may arrive singing.

In the darkness of midwinter, when seasonal song and flickering light shows offer their vestigial reminders of angelic beings, we may find ourselves newly drawn toward tales of divine encounter. We may gaze out at stars and wonder what occupies the space through which their light travels. We may not get answers, or audible voices, but if we pause and gaze and listen, we may find that the very quality of attention we bring to the possibility of Presence changes our awareness. Winter darkness invites inwardness. If we go in rather than on, we may discover within us a chamber where something ancient and assuring resonates—an affirmation, a promise, a celebration, an invitation—is poured out, limitless and patient, bidden or unbidden, for us to hear when we're ready, and join in.

A Broken House

Wind whistling, as it does
in winter, and I think
nothing of it until
it snaps a shutter off
her bedroom window, spins
it over the roof and down
to crash on the deck in back,
like something out of Oz.
We look up, stunned—then glad
to be safe and have a story,
characters in a fable
we only half-believe.
Look, in my surprise
I somehow split a wall,
the last one in the house
we're making of gingerbread.
We'll have to improvise:
prop the two halves forward
like an open double door
and with a tube of icing

cement them to the floor.
Five days until Christmas,
and the house cannot be closed.
When she peers into the cold
interior we've exposed,
she half-expects to find
three magi in the manger,
a mother and her child.
She half-expects to read
on tablets of gingerbread
a line or two of Scripture,
as she has every morning
inside a dated shutter
on her Advent calendar.
She takes it from the mantel
and coaxes one fingertip
under the perforation,
as if her future hinges
on not tearing off the flap
under which a thumbnail picture
by Raphael or Giorgione,
Hans Memling or David
of apses, niches, archways,
cradles a smaller scene
of a mother and her child,
of the lidded jewel-box
of Mary's downcast eyes.
Flee into Egypt, cries
the angel of the Lord
to Joseph in a dream,

for Herod will seek the young
child to destroy him. While
she works to tile the roof
with shingled peppermints,
I wash my sugared hands
and step out to the deck
to lug the shutter in,
a page torn from a book
still blank for the two of us,
a mother and her child.

—Mary Jo Salter, "Advent"

Motherhood is hard to rescue from popular sentimentalities that sugar over the fierce, aching need to protect children even as you face, and know they have to face, howling winds and worse. It is hard, even when danger has come and gone—a heavy shutter ripped off and crashed safely outside a child's window—not to imagine what might have been, not to feel the chill of retroactive horror at injury averted.

The sense of safety that reasserts itself after the flying missile has come to rest is a little more precarious; each time we are reminded—those of us who care for children—how little lies between them and harm. We are reminded momentarily to imagine those mothers whose children do face or suffer harm, who stare from the rubble of bombed buildings or cover their ears at the roar of bulldozers at work destroying their homes. Maybe we are relieved to have been spared—"to be safe and have a story." Yet something has changed, an awareness has formed.

In the story this poem tells, the moment of danger doesn't pass without consequence: The gingerbread house is broken. It is a small forfeit: Far better that little loss than the greater damage that came so close. Repair requires ingenuity. A wall becomes two open doors and the interior is opened to reimagining. A broken house becomes a place where an ancient story might have—might still—take place.

In even smaller spaces, behind smaller shutters, easily torn, that ancient tale is told again, and again by artists who have also, in their own dark winters, imagined their way into a stable where a mother, amazed, may already have known the prophet's dark warning: "A sword will pierce your heart."

The little images in the Advent calendar split that story like light in a prism, each rendering a new way of coming to terms with the paradoxes of sacrificial gift, divine humanity, virgin mother, vulnerable God. And in our ordinary moments we are stopped, sometimes stunned, by the small catastrophes that remind us of our own vulnerability.

We take shelter in the stories that draw us into familiar spaces and equip us to face, again, a world of possibilities and of practical necessities that keep us grounded on "this fragile earth, our island home." In the shadow of those stories, we can emerge into the uncertainties of winter weather, lug in whatever weighty thing has befallen us, and continue life in domestic blessing, making repairs, supplying peppermints and icing, knowing the safety we enjoy is both ultimate and provisional.

Maybe It's an Angel

Some days I notice angels everywhere—
light glancing through windows, flying
through stained glass as if through air.
A human ear shaped like a wing,
curiously curving to admit a flare
of sound, tells me of angels listening
to my listening, even as I sing.
What is that vagrant cloud, that glistening?
Often in the blue of heaven a trail
of light from a plane to me appears
as a heavenly body playing there
beyond my grasping. Or, at night, the tail-
light of a truck sends a red spark
like some twinkly being in the dark
trailing her glory robe in sight
of stationary sightseers. Yesterday, morning light
and over the marsh a winged flight,
another view—Gabriel, or a Great Blue?
But often, nightly, through the skylight

stars multiply like silver sand. And near to far
I link myself again with, Oh—there!
One bright, angelic, particular star.

—Luci Shaw, "Angels Everywhere"

We look for light. It's as natural an instinct as seeking water sources or breathing more deeply in forest spaces. We seek it because we need it. In midwinter, light often comes without warmth, reflected on snow with almost unbearable brightness, or gleaming in icicles or diffusing onto frosted windows. Light without heat reminds us how far we live from its burning source on our "darkling plain."

I used to ask writing students to list "things light does." It shines and dazzles. It glistens and bends and oozes. Sometimes, as Luci Shaw notes, it glances through windows and bears angels on its beams.

The poem is not simply fanciful. It admits to a state of mind many of us enter now and then, perhaps when our minds "wander" off chosen paths into open spaces of possibility. Or perhaps when the sentinels of rationality are sleeping and we find ourselves musing about subtleties—light beyond the visible spectrum, what hums in the silence, what flickers just outside peripheral vision, what slight adjustment of the eye's angle it might take to spot an angel—one of those we may be entertaining unaware in the room where a moment ago we seemed to be alone.

So many stories about encounters with angels have appeared in print and on podcasts in recent years, they've become almost commonplace, though also, if we believe them, astonishing. Some come as ordinary people who show up, shield a child from sudden danger, and then, inexplicably, disappear. Some are invisible presences, felt but not seen, who offer comfort or guidance in a moment of desolation. Some come in dreams. Some are visible to the willing eye as shimmering pillars of light. However we receive these stories, whether we hospitably include them well within the realm of the credible or filter the plausible from the unlikely, or are inclined to dismiss them but for the fact that a witness we trust insists they're true, they affect us.

That there may be, could be, are likely to be, or certainly are beings with subtle bodies hanging around to help us is a thought we can't help but entertain now and then. We know insects can see light further out on the spectrum than our eyes detect. We know dogs hear sounds beyond what our own ears can get to. We know subatomic particles with strange names behave strangely. We know, as more and more physicists have acknowledged, that there are more things in heaven and earth than are dreamed of in our philosophies or our physics texts.

So why not angels? And why not take it all personally, as this poet does, scanning the skyscape for a visitor with a name, and linking herself to "one bright, angelic, particular star." Gerard Manley Hopkins, gazing into the same sky in 1877 began "The Starlight Night," with the lovely, childlike summoning, "Look at the stars! look, look up at the skies! / O look at all the fire-folk sitting in the air!" Personification, for him, for Luci Shaw, for most children, many poets, and, now and then, for us, may be more than a poetic device. It may be a way of recognizing a truth that can't be told in cold, objective, rational language: that Presence is everywhere. That we are witnessed. That the ones who witness are "clothed in light, as with a garment." They hover and hum and play and, when we finally quiet our busy selves, "listen to our listening."

A Deepening Roar

Where had I heard this wind before
Change like this to a deeper roar?
What would it take my standing there for,
Holding open a restive door,
Looking down hill to a frothy shore?
Summer was past and the day was past.
Sombre clouds in the west were massed.
Out on the porch's sagging floor,
Leaves got up in a coil and hissed,
Blindly struck at my knee and missed.
Something sinister in the tone
Told me my secret must be known:
Word I was in the house alone
Somehow must have gotten abroad,
Word I was in my life alone,
Word I had no one left but God.

—Robert Frost, "Bereft"

Among all the helpful reflections written about grief in recent decades, Frost's "Bereft" remains one of the most powerful. It is not a comforting poem. It is set as "bleak midwinter" sets in—a season whose challenges New Englanders, like others in their latitude, take seriously: it is a strenuous, treacherous time of year, possibly deadly. Rainer Maria Rilke strikes a similar note of apprehension to Frost's in his poem, "Autumn Day," in which the coming of winter is heralded with a foreboding prophecy:

> Whoever has no house now, will never have one.
> Whoever is alone will stay alone,
> will sit, read, write long letters through the evening,
> and wander the boulevards, up and down,
> restlessly, while the dry leaves are blowing.

Who, if it were avoidable, would choose such lonely confinement? We read poems like these not for consolation, but for the assurance they offer that our most private sufferings, fears, unspecified anxieties are part of the common lot. In them we recognize our own moments of wondering: "Where had I heard this wind before . . .?"

The question reflects the way feelings sometimes outrun our conscious understanding of the moments we inhabit. The mood of the speaker in "Bereft" strikes a familiar note for many of us who have found ourselves unsettled, especially as weather shifts portend change that defies prediction. All he describes— the looming clouds, the sound of wind, the swirl of leaves—is the stuff of an ordinary early winter day. But the wind's roar is deepening; the door, swaying against the wind is restive; the clouds are somber; the porch sags; and the leaves—those same leaves which children might so recently have leaped into with delight—get up in a coil and hiss.

We are subject to forces at work within and around us of which we are only able to take very partial account. What Dylan Thomas identified as "the force that through the green fuse drives the flower" is the same force that moves across this "sinister" land-scape, leaving the speaker acutely aware of his loneliness and vulnerability. It is not only an impersonal property of changing climatic conditions, but something that moves within and beyond him and delivers an encrypted message: you are seen; your secrets are known; your only hope lies in God—perhaps the very God you have managed to avoid in the insulation of human company.

But to have "no one left but God" may, after all, be good news. Driven into a wintery wilderness, the speaker has no recourse, any more than Ezekiel or Job did, but to hear the voice in the whirlwind and reckon with his own spiritual nakedness. He takes the message personally: word must have gotten out and now he is being sought out. This is not Lear on the heath, half-crazed and defiant, but a man who, finding himself alone, finds himself in the hands of a Spirit who blows "where it will," portentous, unsettling, and full of the "harder hope" that refuses false comfort.

Good Trouble

One winter I lived north, alone
and effortless, dreaming myself
into the past. Perhaps, I thought,
words could replenish privacy.
Outside, a red bicycle froze
into form, made the world falser
in its white austerity. So much
happens after harvest: the moon
performing novelty: slaughter,
snow. One hour the same
as the next, I held my hands
or held the snow. I was like sculpture,
forgetting or, perhaps, remembering
everything. Red wings in the snow,
red thoughts ablaze in the war
I was having with myself again.
Everything I hate about the world
I hate about myself, even now
writing as if this were a law

of nature. Say there were deer
fleet in the snow, walking out
the cold, and more gingkoes
bare in the beggar's grove. Say
I was not the only one who saw
or heard the trees, their diffidence
greater than my noise. Perhaps
the future is a tiny flame
I'll nick from a candle. First, I'm burning.
Then, numb. Why must every winter
grow colder, and more sure?

—Jennifer Chang, "The World"

As we've seen repeatedly in these pages, not all poems reassure.
Some reflect, with unsettling accuracy, our uncertainties or appre-
hensions. Some give voice to the hardest things. Auden's "Stop
All the Clocks," for instance, memorably, vigorously puts words
to the outrage that is an all too often unacknowledged dimen-
sion of grief. Sometimes, paradoxically, that is exactly what pain
demands—words that suffice. Words that don't soften or modify
or mollify, but faithfully mirror what must be seen and named
before we can find a way back to health or peace or resilience.

Jennifer Chang's "The World" recalls a bleak winter spent alone
in a snowy place, stilled into inactivity except for "red thoughts
ablaze" in her troubled mind. Wherever she looks, she sees
"falsity": the newness of the moon is a performance; the red bike
turned into white sculpture; the speaker herself seems to freeze
into sculpted form, and into a numbness in which remembering

and forgetting become indistinguishable. Hatred of the world blends into self-hatred. The act of writing itself elicits self-reflexive dismissiveness, as though it simply inscribes false certainties. The future appears fragile as a candle flame, easily extinguished. The return of winter seems to promise nothing but numbness.

In the middle of this litany of somber memories and forebodings, however, the speaker pauses to speculate: say there were deer nearby, or ginkgoes—other living beings who heard the muffled sound of muted trees. And say the quiet around those living beings grew greater than her "noise." Say she was not alone, but found herself among other orders of being, all of them listening. A flicker of hope lies in the mere capacity to imagine.

And the poem itself in its play with words and line breaks, its patterning of experience, its small, skillful poetic devices, is a consent to life, even in its most baffling and burdensome seasons. The protagonist of Samuel Beckett's obliquely comic "Malone Dies" writes from a bed where he is confined, in a hospital or a prison—we're not sure which—with a stubby pencil that might at any time give out. What he writes about seems of no particular consequence, but the writing itself keeps him alive. Words are his lifeline. They may be a nearly ridiculous diminishment of the long tradition of human lament, but they do insist, "I am still here."

Chang's poem, suggestively entitled "The World" rather than "My Bleak Winter," insists as well. The speaker is not only still here, but still reaching out and sharing the hard things with a "world" in which hard things happen to all of us in some bleak season. It tells a painful truth about what winter in fact brings for many: not holiday festivity or piety, not the romance of a "white

Christmas" or the gaiety of family gatherings but, for some, fresh waves of grief, exhaustion, depression that now has a clinical name: "seasonal affective disorder."

The "Blue Christmas" service mentioned earlier in this book, traditionally on the longest night of the year, is held specifically for those who have suffered loss, who are facing their own or a loved one's death, who are living with the absence of partners deployed into dubious battle, or who have simply found the year's news overwhelming and their faith flattened by the weight of a world that has, as Matthew Arnold put it, "neither joy nor love nor light, / nor certitude, nor peace, nor help for pain. . . ." The purpose of Blue Christmas is to acknowledge lament. The service makes hospitable space for sorrow, refusing on all comers' behalf all false hope and even the innocent pleasures of festivity, driving those who gather in grief to the heart of hope itself—the promise of what lies beyond a vale of tears that to some may look endless.

We need those spaces. We need the psalms of lament and the stories of those who have suffered deep depression or disorientation, pain, confusion, discouragement, or simply world weariness. We need the whole story. Without Lear's utter humiliation, no luminous moment of forgiveness. Without poems about the costs of war we fight, no triumphalist rhetoric.

This poem has a long lineage in literary efforts to find words for what we suffer, when we think we are alone. But, it acknowledges, simply by being a poem, that we are not alone. We can speak into the daunting winter silences and, listening, hear wind in bare branches and, watching, find that other creatures are listening too.

Winter of Discontent

Boston snowbound, Logan closed, snowplows
and salt-trucks flashing yellow, drifts
tall as a man some places, visibility poor,
I sit by the window and watch the snow
blow sideways north-northeast, hot cup
in hand, robe over pajamas.
You have made me to seek refuge
and charged me to care for my brothers.
How cruel. That could be You out there
howling, cracking the trees, burying everything.
What could I possibly want from You
that would not undo the whole world as it is?
                              —Richard Hoffman, "Winter Psalm"

Bless the psalmist who left us a legacy of complaint. Mingled
with praise, this psalm leaves us a record of complex, exuberant
piety that makes ample room for impatience, disappointment,

bewilderment, sorrow, and full-throated anger as well as profound delight and gratitude. Some of the more unsettling biblical psalms are in lockstep, even whiny: "Why do the wicked prosper?" (37:7) or, more directly, "O God, listen to my complaint." (64:1)

Richard Hoffman's poem is just this kind of prayer. It's bitter cold in the Boston streets, noisy machinery has been deployed to clear deep banks of snow in the urban streets, air travel has come to a halt, and all the inconveniences of mid-winter are oppressing the spirits of the speaker, bundled and gazing bleakly out the window. The poem could just have been a wry ode to midwinter in the lineage of Keats's "To Autumn," but when the poet brings God into it, the ante goes up. When complaint becomes prayer it moves into paradox, a defining feature of the holy.

In this poem, as in much of Emily Dickinson's poetry, God appears as a divine adversary—the one who invents the daunting challenges we are admonished to meet and solve, generously, inventively, providing for our brothers and sisters even as we ourselves are driven to "seek refuge." In what might be one of her most religiously cheeky poems, Dickinson addresses this harsh deity with bitter sarcasm: "We apologize to thee / for thine own Duplicity."

The last stanza of Hoffman's poem sounds a slightly different note. The speaker begins with a shocking moment of turning, a little like the "volta" in one of Donne's Holy Sonnets, which deliver some shocking theological blows to sentimental piety. "How cruel," the speaker says. The two words are followed by a period, not an exclamation point that might make them another whine. Here they are more like a cold, detached observation. If we are to recognize in the forces of nature, he reasons, we have to reckon with a God who will howl, crack the trees, and "bury everything." Winter at its least habitable brings up its own unsettling questions about the divine intelligence behind the design. The final lines drop us into a sudden profound question about our prayers, and behind them the desires of our small and curious hearts: "What could I possibly want from You / that would not undo the whole world as it is?"

We can read those lines either as a bitter indictment of the God who seems to have made human lives unnecessarily difficult or as a sudden, humble recognition that if we received the relief we pray for, it might be an unraveling of far more than we imagine.

Scientists, mystics, visionaries, and occasionally poets have traced some of the intricate lines of connection among beings and forces in the created order. We are interdependent in ways we can barely begin to fathom. All that lives and moves and has being—the seasons of sun and snow, animals who hibernate or migrate to survive, plants that go dormant or return to frozen soil when winter comes, and humans who huddle in shelters too often inadequate, depending on their "brothers" to help them—are somehow gathered under the shadow of wings that sometimes can seem like those of a raptor. Still, the self-focused narratives that inform our prayers in the winters of our discontent very likely miss the much larger point: How, this poet asks, would we know what to ask for that wouldn't be our own undoing?

The good news is that we are somehow made in such a way as to be able to see and revise, to change, to grasp that our journeys are part of a much larger story, and ultimately give thanks, even for the season's harshest blessings.

Gratitude After All

Sundays too my father got up early
and put his clothes on in the blueblack cold,
then with cracked hands that ached
from labor in the weekday weather made
banked fires blaze. No one ever thanked him.

I'd wake and hear the cold splintering, breaking.
When the rooms were warm, he'd call,
and slowly I would rise and dress,
fearing the chronic angers of that house,

Speaking indifferently to him,
who had driven out the cold
and polished my good shoes as well.
What did I know, what did I know
of love's austere and lonely offices?
                    —Robert Hayden, "Those Winter Sundays"

The lovely, poignant phrase that ends this poem has been a gift to me, as it has to several generations of readers who have found themselves, as they pause over the final line, remembering how little they, too, understood, as self-interested adolescents, "love's austere and lonely offices." The way confession and gratitude converge here rings true. Much of our gratitude is belated. The moments of reframing that come in occasional retrospection often come by means of very specific memories. For the speaker in this poem, it is the memory of his father lighting the fire on winter mornings. Not a memory of the fire's warmth, or of the comfort it gave, but of what it cost the man with cracked and aching hands who rose into "blueblack cold" to light it.

The tribute the poem offers to a father's fidelities is not uncomplicated. Only one line acknowledges how the speaker (and, as we know, the poet) feared "the chronic angers of that house," but it sets the context for a story, largely untold, of how love survives. Trauma, abuse, neglect, harsh words, or chill silences can sometimes snuff it out, but remarkably often it flickers back into life in healing reflection. Compassion itself is austere; it can grow from the smallest moments of remembering, ignited sometimes by a single image—a cracked hand or polished shoes.

Hayden himself grew up poor and often in pain from the confusion of parents' hostilities and foster parents' stop-gap care. Detroit in wintertime must have been then, as it must still be now, a harsh place to be poor. Adequate heat is a luxury to be meted out sparingly by those whose hours of poorly paid labor doubles the price they pay for it. Winter brings many of us to its own terms with the cost of living. I think of Emily Dickinson's unsettling description of the deadening numbness of cold in her poem about what it is to live with the irremediable fact of pain: "First—Chill—then Stupor—then the letting go –." It doesn't take much, according to those who report having been very near death by cold, to reach that tipping point where the body simply stops trying to warm itself. It takes a great deal, on the other hand, to keep the fire in the hearth, the fire in the body, the fire in the spirit burning in the dead of winter. That familiar phrase reminds us that death comes a little closer in wintertime and is more visible.

The speaker in this poem knows that chill and knows now what kept him alive in the dead of winter. The harshness of his father's task is mirrored in the "splintering" and "breaking," probably of wood, though in the poem it is the cold itself that is broken, giving the father's life-giving work a mythic dimension. Only now can he remember those winters with gratitude. The gratitude is laced with regret: "No one ever thanked him."

He invites readers to personal reflection, whatever their winter morning may have been: Who got you through the winter? Who kept you warm? Whose work gave you rest? Who attended to your small needs—or your large ones—in the most challenging seasons? What austere and lonely offices must someone have performed on your behalf? It's good for all of us to take the measure of what has been provided, best if we do it in reviewing the concrete particulars of our own winter mornings and in small reminders like the smell of freshly polished shoes.

Due Regard

One must have a mind of winter
To regard the frost and the boughs
Of the pine-trees crusted with snow;

And have been cold a long time
To behold the junipers shagged with ice,
The spruces rough in the distant glitter

Of the January sun; and not to think
Of any misery in the sound of the wind,
In the sound of a few leaves,

Which is the sound of the land
Full of the same wind
That is blowing in the same bare place

For the listener, who listens in the snow,
And, nothing himself, beholds
Nothing that is not there and the nothing that is.

—Wallace Stevens, "The Snow Man"

Wallace Stevens's poems are notoriously difficult for most readers when they first encounter them. His experiments with point of view, syntax, phrasing, paradox, and logic make some of them— "The Snow Man," for instance—read like riddles. Like a riddle, this poem invites us to reframe what we see on a snowy winter day and, beyond that, to reconsider how we see what we see. The speaker assumes an unabashedly instructive posture: if we are really to regard—or to put it more precisely, to give due regard—to the snow in the trees in winter, we *must* "have a mind of winter." Seeing adequately or rightly—regarding—requires something of us. We owe something to those parts of the world we routinely reduce to objects. Indeed, to regard them, we need to identify with them—imagine what it is to be like them, think from their point of view, even if that seems a fanciful exercise.

The word "regard" carries layers of meaning from earlier centuries: to protect; to confer value; to respect; to watch. It suggests a deeply relational way of seeing. What might it mean to see all creatures in their terms rather than ours? To consider what it's like to be winter, or to be a pine in snow or a juniper in ice? A spruce in January sun? And not to project our human feelings, but to empty ourselves of those in order to imagine what it might be like to be alive in another life form?

The wind that blows across barren fields fills our lungs. It moves through us; we are part of the landscape it touches. When we pause, say, on a winter day, to notice that connection, we may come to realize that, as many have said in moments of spiritual epiphany, we are one with all of it—the whole created order. All that has life and breath. All that is made of molecules moved by the same forces. The repetition of "nothing" in the final stanza recalls both Buddhist and Christian ideas of "self-emptying": only when we are empty of ego, when we have "lost" the life we cling to, when, as Auden put it, our "dream of safety" disappears, can we, in that "nothingness," see truly, seeing nothing that is not there: no projections, no superimposition of personal memory or desire, no speculation or regret—just seeing what is. And finally, once we get to that place of seeing nothing that is not there, we might, the poem suggests, be prepared to see "the nothing that is"—openness, emptiness, mystery. Though I have no reason to think he made this connection, the attention Stevens gives to "the nothing" that may be beheld only by means of a shift of consciousness reminds me of the prayer, "In thy light may we see light." Light is what we see by. Seeing the light—the daylight around us, the light that bounces off the retina, the light some see in human auras—involves reversing ground and field so that objects are backgrounded and the light itself can become the object of our gaze. The prayer suggests that only those who see with eyes of faith may be enabled to "see the light." Emptied of self, filled with the life force of divine love, we may assume some among us have in fact seen "nothing that is not there" and "the nothing that is," and have learned, in winter, to enter "the mind of winter," laying aside, perhaps for a January afternoon, all that clutters what one mystic I know has called "the knowing field."

Out of Ordinary Time

The threefold terror of love; a fallen flare
Through the hollow of an ear;
Wings beating about the room;
The terror of all terrors that I bore
The Heavens in my womb.
Had I not found content among the shows
Every common woman knows,
Chimney corner, garden walk,
Or rocky cistern where we tread the clothes
And gather all the talk?
What is this flesh I purchased with my pains,
This fallen star my milk sustains,
This love that makes my heart's blood stop
Or strikes a Sudden chill into my bones
And bids my hair stand up?

—W. B. Yeats, "Mother of God"

If there is an obvious place in the liturgical year for Yeats's stirring meditation on the "Mother of God," it is the day the church celebrates the Annunciation—Gabriel's visit to Mary, her consent, the beginning (so we imagine, though deep beginnings are always prior) of Christian history. But that moment intrudes into the songs and carols of Advent as months of hiddenness come to an end and the birth that is to change everything happens.

Whether you are among those who believe in the literal virgin birth of Jesus or among those who dismiss it as a fiction, or somewhere in between, that story has provided a powerful focus over the centuries for reflection and conversation, art and poetry, theology, and even social theory. It asks us to imagine a God humble enough to become a helpless infant in the care of a peasant girl; the presence and power of angels—beings of other orders—who teach and guide and guard human lives, occasionally emerging from obscurity to bring the earthly and heavenly realms together; the power behind the Big Bang, the intelligence that shaped the universe and scattered the stars concentrated in a naked baby lying in a feeding trough—as T. S. Eliot put it, "word within a word, unable to speak a word."

The story that takes us from Mary's shocking encounter with the angel Gabriel to Jesus's birth reminds us that faith, love, and wisdom call us into perpetual paradox, where ultimate safety feels a lot like danger; revelation deepens mystery; and love is a "threefold terror." Mary is baffled. Joseph is afraid. The villagers are suspicious. Shepherds quake. The great feasts of the Christian calendar call us out of "ordinary time" into a state of mind and imagination and awareness that insists on something truer and larger than what the five senses can verify. Words like "wondrous," or more ancient words, "O Magnum Mysterium," make space in our consciousness for what we cannot fully understand.

Sometimes the incomprehensible thing is also deeply personal. It may be that only Mary can say "I bore the Heavens in my womb," but surely every parent who has gazed at a small new stranger who wasn't and now is knows something of that awe. And if we are to credit even a fraction of the huge body of human testimony, increasingly well documented, that angels appear, that prayer shifts things, that near-death experiences offer a foretaste of more to come, we have to—and get to—live with the same questions Yeats raises in this deeply empathetic poem: What is this love that makes my heart's blood stop? What is it that breaks through all my defenses, all my manageable ideas, all my habits and efforts to contain and control, and, now and then, "strikes a sudden chill into my bones and bids my hair stand up?"

It is not Mary's elevated, canonized status as Queen of Heaven we see in this poem, but a fearful human being whose moment for divine encounter has come. I believe we all get those—some more dramatic than others. And if, when they come, we manage to say yes, we may find what lies on the other side of fear and go on to live lives of radical amazement.

Living on the Cusp

This was the moment when Before
Turned into After, and the future's
Uninvented timekeepers presented arms.

This was the moment when nothing
Happened. Only dull peace
Sprawled boringly over the earth.

This was the moment when even energetic Romans
Could find nothing better to do
Than counting heads in remote provinces.

And this was the moment
When a few farm workers and three
Members of an obscure Persian sect
Walked haphazard by starlight straight
Into the kingdom of heaven.

—U. A. Fanthorpe, "BC:AD"

One of W. H. Auden's most often quoted lines, always with a smile, reminds us how "the dogs go on with their doggy life and the torturer's horse / Scratches its innocent behind on a tree" even as something momentous—world-changing—is taking place nearby. In the same spirit, Fanthorpe reminds us that this is, in fact, how the greatest things happen: inconspicuously, unnoticed at first, like a seed breaking underground or a tectonic plate shifting or a fissure widening one last millimeter. Or a child born to poor parents in occupied territory. And a "few farm workers and three members of an obscure Persian sect" follow a summons no one else hears and show up to celebrate a peasant baby's midnight birth. The big things happen in ordinary moments. In an instant an egg is fertilized, a door opens, a last breath is drawn, a nod is given. A bewildered girl sees an angel, perhaps looking like an ordinary man, and says yes.

"Momentous" shares a root with its opposite, "momentary." In the moment we don't know which is which. Significance is assigned in retrospect, or already assigned from "the foundations of the earth," each thing happening in "the fullness of time" as a result of forces set in motion in the stillness of empty space, unhistoric and unwitnessed except by the One who knew what would come to pass and said "let there be," and there was.

In the waiting season of Advent Christians look back over a calendar year of history nearly completed and forward to the "high holiday" that marks a moment in a story so long in the making, its opening line can only be "in the beginning." When it comes it will be "the moment when Before turned into After." Yes. And.

Every moment is that moment. Before turns into After. We hover between the two at the "still point of the turning world," in the timeless "already and not yet" that is always hidden just behind a veil of time. The busyness, even of those who mark the season as sacred, protects them from all but the merest flickerings of a mystery whose magnitude is unimaginable and unendurable, but for the grace of incarnation.

Grace happens in the midst of political squalor and sloth. Miracles happen in the midst of things to those willing to drop their nets or leave their sheep or books and follow guidance they can't account for. Still. "History is being made," we occasionally hear at an inauguration or a site dedication or the signing of a bill. Even as we celebrate those moments, it's good to remember how history unfolds quietly—as Auden puts it, "while someone else is eating or opening a window or just walking dully along," and while disengaged bureaucrats count heads in remote provinces— and it's good to be watchful.

That watchfulness is the challenge of Advent: watch for flicker- ings of divine light. Watch for where grace happens. Watch for the subtle summonings that might lead you, if you're willing, haphazard into the kingdom of heaven.

Awakening Song

O God of words and music, we give thanks
for psalms and hymns and spiritual songs
connecting us to long-ago believers.
We thank you, Lord of sound and harmony,
for the Church's many voices raised in praise.
Sing your Spirit in our hearts and voices,
that our gratitude might brim and overflow.
        —Diane Tucker, "One Winter—Forty New O Antophons"

I know (and love) a boy who doesn't like to sing. He has other great virtues. But his aversion to singing, and his conviction that it is an unnecessary occupation, sometimes, indeed, a waste of valuable time, makes me sad. I hope a song will awaken him sometime to joy that couldn't come any other way—a direct infusion from the "God of words and music" who sings to us and through us. It probably won't be "Have Yourself a Merry Little Christmas." It might be "In the Bleak Midwinter."

Song is irreducible. With the benefit of YouTube, most of us now can hear boy choir voices from English cathedrals or monks chanting in Tibet or spirited African dancers intoning "Baba Yetu"—Our Father—in Swahili to the beat of skin drums. Changes in the way we use communication technology, triggered by the recent pandemic, have made possible composite choirs from around the world—one of them seventeen thousand voices intoning "Sing gently as one." What we receive from each of them we could not make for ourselves—connection to the "long-ago believers" who, if they followed Paul's explicit instructions, addressed one another "in psalms and hymns and spiritual songs, singing and making melody to the Lord" (Ephesians 5:19) and to ancestors who sang to their children who sang the same songs to theirs.

The music we share attunes us to one another. We "fall in step" with others on the paths we travel. We sway with them at concerts and are lifted into a new state of mind by the sheer energy of blended voices. A thicket of voices summons us for at least the duration of a song out of the entrenchments that divide us and into an energy field that can be, some moments, transformative—certainly when we are participants, but also when we listen. One voice, one flute, one drumbeat might, on the other hand, be all it takes to change the mood of an afternoon or awaken us into gratitude or allow us to be comforted.

It's almost pointless to embark on a justification of music; it's like an apologia for breathing. We do it because we must. We do it despite ourselves. We do it because if we didn't, even the stones would cry out. (Chinese "stone medicine" suggests they already do, along with trees that "clap their hands" and hills that "sing for joy.") I learned a few years ago from a colleague in computer science that some are concluding everything is made of "information." We've known for a long time that everything in the universe vibrates. The medieval idea of the "music of the spheres," produced by celestial bodies and perfectly harmonious, seems quite plausible to me. We live in music the way we live in light.

So, in a season when choirs and choruses around the world are once again singing carols or Handel's *Messiah* or high liturgies or even "White Christmas," it's a good time to address our prayers to the God of music who, in words that must have been the original melody, sang us, and all that is, into being.

The Force of Peace

Peace is the centre of the atom, the core
Of quiet within the storm. It is not
A cessation, a nothingness; more
The lightning in reverse is what
Reveals the light. It is the law that binds
The atom's structure, ordering the dance
Of proton and electron, and that finds
Within the midst of flame and wind, the glance
In the still eye of the vast hurricane.
Peace is not placidity: peace is
The power to endure the megatron of pain
With joy, the silent thunder of release,
The ordering of Love. Peace is the atom's start,
The primal image: God within the heart.
                    —Madeleine L'Engle, "Sonnet, Trinity 18"

Peace is where we start from. In the quiet, dark, secret places of the womb we are "knit together." One microscopic encounter zips tiny chains of DNA together and we begin our embodied lives as earthlings. The understanding of peace L'Engle invites in this sonnet is electric, astonishing. "The power to endure the megatron of pain / with joy" brings vividly to mind people I've known whose lot it was to live with daily grinding aches and who did so, not as victims nor in denial of it, but with equanimity—and occasionally real joy—mined from the deepest reaches of their will.

For several years, I found myself in close encounters with Quakers. Among the many habits of mind I learned from them was this: that pacifism, or peacemaking, is the furthest thing from passivity. Dedicated pacifists and peacemakers work hard and bravely to promote understanding that leads to action—prison reform, conflict resolution, disarmament. Traditional Quakers, like Buddhists, greet one another with acknowledgment of the "Light within"—the "God within the heart" L'Engle identifies here as a force that shapes, reveals, and releases—one might almost say detonates something thunderous and uncontained.

Or else it is a force intensified in its containment. Nuclear force binds protons and neutrons together at the center of the atom, making it stable. Unleashed, that force cascades and expands. At peace, it enables things to be what they are. Each mortal thing, shaped and structured and stabilized, cries, Hopkins writes, "What I do is me: for that I came." That peace, which L'Engle locates at the center of the atom at the center of the heart, Hopkins reminds us, "indoors each one dwells." We have within us the seeds of peace. Nuclear physics may explain how subatomic particles cohere, but there is, within and beyond those barely observable elements of being, something that still "passeth understanding." It is ours to draw on—a gift and a birthright, buried in the accretion and accumulation of growth, but available when we return to center.

Those who practice centering prayer, those who find their balance points in yoga or dance, those who sing from the solar plexus or wait and watch for the hurtling ball, ready to move in any direction, know that moment of peace when all is "hung in the balance" and one's power is gathered and ready and open and unafraid. From that place, what comes forth may surprise even the one from whose body it swells and breaks. At our best we are vessels and channels. What we allow to move through us is our best gift to the world. We bear it—sometimes "endure" it—often without knowing its extent or object. It is ours to allow. The rest, as Eliot bluntly put it, "is not our business."

Opening a Way

I asked you
where
does the white of the snow
go after it is gone?

then you said
look,
I want to show you this
   light
   take my hands
   let go
          —Melanie Poli, "And Fear Shall Be No More"

Relinquishment frees us. When we let go, something is set free. The turning of each season releases us into the changed light of the next. The last day of summer, the last leaf-fall before the tree is fully bare, and, later, the last snowmelt enact the letting go that makes way again and again for what is next.

Winter, more than other seasons, seems a time of letting go. Especially as it begins, for those who live where weather changes most dramatically, coming and going require more effort and more preparation. Summer clothing is put away, the flexibilities of long days give way to more stringent enclosure and earlier dusk. For those living on the economic margins, cold is colder and warmth more expensive. Relinquishments are measurable, daunting, and sometimes scary.

But in this lovely poem, whose title is a promise, we are reminded how loss may open the way for light. What goes doesn't just disappear, but dissolves into a new medium. As the white of the snow returns to light and ice to earth and air, so whatever transitory beauties we delight in will melt into memory and in their place light will remain.

We receive them, the poet reminds us, from the hand of their, and our, Creator. As they come and go—the glistening snow, the crocus, the blooming tree, the waves, the flaming leaves, the harvest—they enact for us again and again the drama of original separation. A child leaves the womb and emerges into her own place on earth, and between her and the womb that held her there is space and light and possibility.

I remember learning to float on water, then to ride a bike, to skate, to drive, to take my place at a podium. Each time there came a moment of letting go, which was also a moment of finding out, finding myself to be freer than I had thought, more agile, more able to trust what I had been given and prepared for. Each time the hand that had held me opened, and I let go.

I like to think of the last lines of this poem as an invitation to prayer in moments of relinquishment: "Look / I want to show you this light / take my hands / let go." If you do, the space around you, which you thought would be empty, will be filled with light and perhaps we will see, as Emerson once insisted, that all things glitter and swim.

Sources

Gene Baro, "Mid-Winter," copyright © Gene Baro. Used by permission.

Jennifer Chang, "The World," copyright © Jennifer Chang. Used by permission.

Billy Collins, "Winter," originally published in *Poetry East*. Used by permission of Billy Collins.

U. A. Fanthorpe, "BC:AD," from *Selected Poems*, published by Enitharmon Press, www.enitharmon.co.uk, reproduced by permission of Dr. R. V. Bailey.

Robert Francis, "Blue Winter," reprinted from *Collected Poems: 1936–1976*. Copyright © 1976 by Robert Francis. Published by the University of Massachusetts Press.

Kinereth Gensler, "December," from *Journey Fruit: Poems and a Memoir*. Copyright © 1997 by Kinereth Gensler. Reprinted with the permission of The Permissions Company LLC, on behalf of Alice James Books, alicejamesbooks.org.

From untitled shaman song "The great sea stirs me . . ." (Uvavnuk), in *Women in Praise of the Sacred* by Jane Hirshfield. Copyright © 1994 by Jane Hirshfield. Used by permission of HarperCollins Publishers.

Linda Gregg, "Winter Love," from *Chosen by the Lion*. Used by permission of Graywolf Press.

Joy Harjo, "Praise the Rain," from *Conflict Resolution for Holy Being*. Copyright © 2015 Joy Harjo. Used by permission of W. W. Norton.

Notes

INVITED INWARD

7 *"All great spirituality teaches about letting go":* Adapted from Richard Rohr, *Essential Teachings on Love*, selected by Joelle Chase and Judy Traeger (Maryknoll, NY: Orbis Books, 2018), 199.

BLUE CHRISTMAS

11 *I think often in this respect of Thomas Hardy's insistence:* Thomas Hardy, "In Tenebris II," in *The Complete Poetical Works of Thomas Hardy*, vol. 1, ed. Samuel Hynes (Oxford: Oxford University Press, 1983).

JUST BEYOND SAFE

19 *The cruise ship* **Disney Wonder** *where, according to the ad:* Disney Cruise Line (website), https://disneycruise.disney.go.com/ships/wonder.

19 *"The sense of danger must not disappear":* W. H. Auden, "Leap Before You Look," in *W. H. Auden: Collected Poems*, edited by Edward Mendelson (New York: Random House, 1976), 244.

LOCAL TRUTHS

23 *"Pain comes from the darkness"*: Randall Jarrell, "90 North," in *The Complete Poems of Randall Jarrell* (New York: Farrar Straus & Giroux, 1981), 113.

24 *"Everything begins here"*: David B. Prather, "Provenance," https://thewildword.com/david-b-prather.

24 *We inhabit eternity, but only because, as T. S. Eliot put it*: T. S. Eliot, "East Coker," in *T. S. Eliot: Collected Poems 1909–1962* (London: Faber & Faber, 1974), 197.

SINGING IN THE COLD

42 *"In the dark times, will there also be singing?"*: Bertold Brecht, "Svenborg Poems," in *Poems 1913–1956*, ed. John Willett, Ralph Manheim, and Erich Fried (London: Eyre Methuen, 1976), 320.

SHADES

54 *Her daughter brings what she can:* Toni Morrison, *Beloved* (New York: Knopf, 1987), 4.

55 *Herman Melville's Ishmael muses:* Herman Melville, *Moby-Dick* (New York: Penguin, 2013), 349.

NOTICINGS

64 *is enhanced and made lovely like T. S. Eliot's roses:* T. S. Eliot, "Burnt Norton," in *T. S. Eliot: Collected Poems*, 190.

INSCRIPTIONS

73 *Mary Oliver's poem, "Mozart, for Example"*: Mary Oliver, "Mozart, for Example," in *Thirst* (Boston: Beacon Press, 2006), 12.

LIVING IN LIGHT

77 *"Look at the stars! Look, look up at the skies!"*: Gerard Manley Hopkins, "The Starlight Night," in *A Hopkins Reader*, ed. John Pick (New York: Doubleday, 1966), 48.

PAST INTO PRESENT

93 *"Nothing is lost"*: Edmund Spenser, *The Faerie Queene*, ed. A. C. Hamilton (London: Longman, 1977), Book V, Canto II, XXXIX, 541.

OTHER BEINGS

96 *Thoreau's insistence that "in wildness is the preservation of the world"*: H. D. Thoreau, "Walking," in *The Norton Book of Nature Writing*, ed. Robert Finch and John Elder (New York: W. W. Norton, 1990), 192.

WHAT THE TREES RELINQUISH

101 *her indigenous people recognize trees . . . as neighbors, givers, protectors:* Robin Wall Kimmerer, *Braiding Sweetgrass* (Minneapolis: Milkweed Editions, 2015).

BEYOND SAFETY

112 *"out of that silence greater than all words"*: T. S. Eliot, "Little Gidding," in *T. S. Eliot: Collected Poems*, 221.

112 *the kind of hope Eliot wrote about:* T. S. Eliot, "East Coker," in *T. S. Eliot: Collected Poems*, 126.

113 *"I had seen birth and death"*: T. S. Eliot, "Journey of the Magi," in *The Complete Poems and Plays 1909–1950* (New York: Harcourt, Brace & World, 1971), 69.

MAYBE IT'S AN ANGEL

125 *Gerard Manley Hopkins, gazing into the same sky in 1877*: Gerard Manley Hopkins, "The Starlight Night," https://www.poetryfoundation. org/poems/44401/the-starlight-night.

A DEEPENING ROAR

128 *"Whoever has no house now, will never have one"*: Rainer Maria Rilke, "Herbsttag," trans. Stephen Mitchell as "Autumn Day," in *The Selected Poetry of Rainer Maria Rilke: Bilingual Edition* (New York: Modern Library, 1995), 15.

GRATITUDE AFTER ALL

141 *"First—Chill—then Stupor—then the letting go -"*: Emily Dickinson, "After Great Pain, a Formal Feeling Comes," in *The Complete Poems of Emily Dickinson*, ed. Thomas H. Johnson (Boston: Little Brown, 1960), 341.

DUE REGARD

145 *as Auden put it, our "dream of safety"*: W. H. Auden, "Leap Before You Look," in *W. H. Auden: Collected Poems*, 244.

OUT OF ORDINARY TIME

148 *"word within a word, unable to speak a word"*: T. S. Eliot, "Gerontion," in *T. S. Eliot: Collected Poems*, 39.

LIVING ON THE CUSP

152 *One of W. H. Auden's most often quoted lines:* W. H. Auden, "Musée des Beaux Arts," in *W. H. Auden: Collected Poems*, 146.

153 *Even as we celebrate those moments, it's good to remember how history unfolds quietly:* Auden, "Musée des Beaux Arts," in *W. H. Auden: Collected Poems*, 146.

THE FORCE OF PEACE

160 *Hopkins writes, "What I do is me: for that I came":* Gerard Manley Hopkins, "As Kingfishers Catch Fire," in *A Hopkins Reader*, ed. John Pick (New York: Image Books, 1966), 67.

161 *The rest, as Eliot bluntly put it:* T. S. Eliot, "East Coker," in *T. S. Eliot: The Complete Poems and Plays*, 128.